When Capone's Mob Murdered Roger Touhy

◆

The Strange Case of Touhy, Jake the Barber and the Kidnapping that Never Happened

When Capone's Mob Murdered Roger Touhy

◆

The Strange Case of Touhy, Jake the Barber and the Kidnapping that Never Happened

John W. Tuohy

BARRICADE
BOOKS

Fort Lee, New Jersey

Published by Barricade Books Inc.
185 Bridge Plaza North
Suite 308-A
Fort Lee, NJ 07024

ISBN: 1-56980-174-6

Library of Congress Cataloging-in-Publication Data
Contact the Library of Congress for this information

Printed in the United States of America.

10 9 8 7 6 5 4 3 2 1

Contents

Note:
The author would like to extend a special thanks to
Betty Brennan, the widow of Roger Touhy's collaborator, Ray Brennan for her input and memory during the research of this book. Her help was immea-
sureable. He also expresses his gratitude to the
memoir written by Touhy and Brennan, *The Stolen
Years*. Without that book, this one would have been
nearly impossible to write.

Everything's got a moral if only you can find it.
—Lewis Carroll

Preface

I began work on this book while I still was an undergraduate student in the Criminal Justice Program at the University of New Haven in 1975. The book grew out of class assignment, given to us by Dr. Henry Lee who later came to some fame as an expert witness during the sensational O.J. Simpson murder trial.

Dr. Lee assigned each of us in the class to investigate and write about a case of a miscarriage of American justice.

I had heard a few, vague facts about the Roger Touhy case from my father, who had heard about it from his father, who had known Roger Touhy. After some initial research, I placed a call to Betty Brennan, the widow of Touhy's ghost writer on his autobiography, *The Stolen Years*.

Betty was a wealth of insightful, important information and she encouraged me to follow up on the case, which I did, not realizing then that the investigation into the true facts behind the Roger Touhy case would take up almost twenty-six years of my life and propel me across the United States, from

Washington to Las Vegas and Los Angeles to Miami and back again, in search of the truth. I interviewed several hundred people and pored over thousands of pages of documents that relate to the case.

After all of that, I am only certain of one thing; no one except Roger Touhy and John Factor really knows the full truth behind this case. However, after tens of thousands of hours of research, there are some aspects of the story which I am certain are true but can't prove. As a result, they have not been included in the main text of this book.

I am certain that Touhy and Factor knew each other before the kidnapping occurred, that Factor probably didn't completely understand that he would never be freed of the Mafia's iron-clad grasp on his life and that Sam Giancana was one of the wheelmen for Touhy's assassins on that frigid December night when the Capone mob killed Touhy.

Which brings us to the title of this book. Although Al Capone had been dead for twelve years by the time Touhy was shot to death, and although the intention of the murder was to silence Touhy forever and was carried out with chilling business-like efficiency, Roger Touhy's murder was personal. His killers had been members of the old 42 Gang and had fought Touhy in Capone's name twenty-six years earlier. The same holds true for the mob bosses who ordered the killing. They had watched as Touhy's Irish gunmen shot their way across the Windy City, murdering their childhood friends, cousins, business partners, and brothers.

I also want to take this opportunity to share my concerns about the secretive and powerful role of the United States Pardon Attorney, which, officially anyway, falls under the Office of the Attorney General of the United States.

In my quest for the truth about President Kennedy's very suspicious twelfth-hour pardon of John Factor, the Pardons Attorney's Office went out of its way to derail my research. Pardon records that I requested as part of this investigation were moved around the country making access difficult, sometimes impossible. On several occasions, records were hidden from me. I was lied to several times regarding the existence of some pardon records and members of my staff were questioned about my personal life.

Still, even with this interference, I uncovered a total of 500 pardons granted by Presidents Truman and Kennedy, which, at the least, can be considered highly questionable. For this reason, I have come to the conclusion that John Factor's presidential pardon was granted as part of the federal government's tangled and illegal dealings with the Mafia during the Kennedy administration.

However, this is the stuff for another researcher and another writer for another book, but the undisputable fact remains that if details of the Factor pardon have not been released, the fault lies squarely with the U.S. Pardons Attorney's Office.

—John William Tuohy
Washington D.C.
March 2001

Introduction

Prohibition ruled America in the 1920s. It produced a lawless decade and lawless citizens. In Chicago, Al Capone became not only the nation's leading bootlegger but a pioneer and kingpin in the union extortion racket, a golden source of easy money and power.

But there was another major crime figure in the Windy City as well, a gangster who emerged from the poverty-drenched Irish slum section known as "the Valley." His name was Roger Touhy, the son of an honest Chicago policeman and the youngest of the six so-called "Terrible Touhy" brothers. Together the six brothers ruled a small but widely-feared criminal empire on the city's outskirts. The gang manufactured and distributed beer, controlled unions and supported their war against the Capones' criminal syndicate through a series of lucrative robberies of the U.S. mail.

This is the story of Roger Touhy's turbulent life.

A career criminal whose underworld deeds were as darkly sensational as Capone's or Luciano's, Touhy evaded both the law and the many attempts on his life by his rivals. However in 1933 he was sentenced to ninety-nine years in prison for a crime he never committed: the kidnapping of international confidence man John "Jake the Barber" Factor.

Factor, the black sheep brother of the cosmetics king, Max Factor, was an illegal immigrant in America, who had fled England to avoid a long jail term for engineering one of the largest stock frauds in the history of the British Empire. In a desperate attempt to save himself from extradition, Factor, working with the Capone organization, had himself kidnapped and, with the connivance of some of Touhy's men, accused Roger Touhy of the crime. After two sensational trials, held in the shadow of the national outrage over the Lindburgh baby kidnapping, Roger was convicted.

After serving eleven years in prison and being denied a hearing for parole, Touhy and a band of convicts shot their way out of Stateville Penitentiary only to be recaptured in a sensational gun battle with the FBI.

Sentenced to an additional ninety-nine years for abetting the escape, Touhy began the long and arduous process of re-opening his case before the federal bench. Finally, seventeen years later, thanks to the efforts of a rumpled private detective and an eccentric lawyer, Roger Touhy won his freedom. A federal judge determined that John Factor had engineered his own kidnapping to avoid extradition.

Freed in 1959, Touhy intended to enter a multi-million-dollar lawsuit against the state of Illinois. After his release from jail he was gunned down on the doorstep of his sister's home. He had been free for twenty-eight days.

John Factor, Touhy's nemesis, was luckier. Over the years he manipulated the legal system through the use of his vast fortune. He managed to remain in the United States but continued to be a pawn for the Chicago mob. In 1955 he ran the incredibly successful Stardust Hotel in Las Vegas, representing the mob and in 1962, just the day before his extradition was ordered, he received a full presidential pardon from John F. Kennedy. He was allowed to remain in the United States, safe from the British courts which had long pursued him.

The Valley

"Roger Touhy," wrote the *Chicago Tribune*, "is one of those rare cases in which the man measured up to the legend."

He was born in a lawless neighborhood called "the Valley." It is gone and largely forgotten now, except by a scant few descendants of the tens of thousands of Irish immigrants who huddled there for a time, making that brutal slum the largest Irish ghetto west of New York.

Located in the heart of Chicago, the Valley was a flat stretch of land partial to winter floods that would fill the water with human waste from the nearby canals. In the summer it was insufferably humid. It was always a dreary place, full of ancient wooden warehouses, overcrowded with stinking tenements, stores with near-empty shelves, and saloons packed with men who had long since given up their dreams of a better life.

Roger Touhy was born there in 1898. He was the last of seven children in one of the thousands of working families jammed into the Valley. While he was still an infant, Roger's mother was burned to death when the kitchen stove exploded. It was a remarkably common occurrence at the time, leaving his father, James, an Irish immigrant and a lowly but otherwise honest beat cop, to raise the family.

"My father," Roger wrote, "was a Chicago policeman. An honest one. Otherwise, he would have had a hell of a lot less trouble getting the grocery and rent money."

James Touhy eventually lost his four eldest sons to a local thug named Paddy "the Bear" Ryan. An enormous hulk of a man, Ryan led the notorious Valley Gang, which was organized in the middle 1860s. It inducted members as young as twelve years of age, and, at least in the beginning, graduated them to the big leagues of crime at around age nineteen or twenty.

In 1870, its membership was mostly made up of the sons of policemen and lower level politicos whose city hall connections kept their sons out of serious trouble with the law. Using that clout, the gang was able to transform itself from a rag-tag group of street urchins who stole fruit off vendors' wagons into a working criminal/political organization.

With time, the gang moved from its basement headquarters on 15th Street to its first official headquarters, a popular saloon on the corner of 14th and Mulberry Streets. From there, the Valley Gang moved into armed robbery and big dollar larceny. But the gang remained a small-time local operation in most respects. Then, in about 1880, the Germans began to move into the Valley, followed by the Jews. The gang terrorized both groups, beating them into submission and coercing cash from their shop owners when extortion became the new money maker.

The gang continued to rule supremely over the Valley until the turn of the century when great masses of Irish, Germans and Jews moved out and were replaced by tens of thousands of southern Italians. Numerically superior and just as tough as the Irish they replaced, the southern Italians were less prone to intimidation than were the Germans and Jews. The Italians had their street gangs as well, some with membership in the hundreds.

Inevitably, street wars between the Irish and the Italians broke out frequently. As a result, the Maxwell Street police station had the highest number of assault and attempted murder cases of any police precinct in the country, outside of Brooklyn. Again, what kept most of the Valley Gang members out of jail were their powerful political contacts, made even stronger by the gang's willingness to rent itself out as polling booth enforcers. However, unlike the smaller street gangs from the Valley—the Beamers, the Plugs and the Buckets of Blood—who also rented out their services, the Valley boys were known for their penchant to switch sides in the middle of a battle if the opposite side was paying more or if it appeared that they might win the election.

By 1910, the gang continued to grow in power in the Valley by having enough sense to allow a limited number of Jews and Germans into its ranks. The Valley Gang remained the largest and deadliest gang in the area and a whole new generation of Irish-American boys in Chicago grew to admire the gang and its leaders "in much the same way" one sociologist wrote, "that other boys looked up to, in a fanciful way, Robin Hood or Jesse James."

By 1919, the Irish had surrendered their majority status in the Valley but managed to retain political control, just as they did throughout most of Chicago as well. By that time, the gang transformed itself into a social and athletic club which, in both

19

votes and money, stood solidly behind several dozen important politicos whose careers had been launched by the gang.

The first important leaders of the Valley Gang were Heinie Miller and Jimmy Farley. Both expert pickpockets and burglars who flourished in the 1900s. Miller and Farley, along with their lieutenants, "Tootsie" Bill Hughes and Bill Cooney (aka "the Fox") were described by the police as "four of the smoothest thieves that ever worked the Maxwell Street district."

Smooth or not, they all went to jail in 1905 for extended stays and the leadership of the gang fell to "Red" Bolton. Bolton's reign was cut short by his own stupidity. He robbed a store in the middle of the Valley, in the middle of the day, killing a cop in the process. No amount of political influence could help. Bolton was sent away to prison where he died of pneumonia in a few years.

With Bolton gone, the gang started to weaken compared to it's previous power, although it had a brief resurgence during the first World War when Chicago was under a temporary alcohol prohibition and the gang went into the rum-running business.

Rum-running brought the gang a lot of money. For the first time, the Valley Boys drove Rolls Royces, wore silk shirts and managed to get out of murder charges by affording the most talented lawyers, including the legendary Clarence Darrow.

In the mid 1890s, when the gang was under the leadership of Paddy the Bear Ryan, the Valley Boys were transformed into labor goons for hire, with the Bear, acting as the salesman, boasting that his boys were the best bomb throwers and acid tossers in the business. The Valley Gang solidified that reputation during the building trades strike of 1900, which put some 60,000 laborers out of work for twenty-six weeks.

Operating under the street command of Walter "Runty" Quinlan, who would eventually lead the gang, the Valley boys terrorized strike breakers with unmerciful beatings and earned their reputation as pro-labor thugs in an age when the bosses and factory owners paid better.

Paddy the Bear ruled the Valley for years and it was the Bear who taught Tommy, Johnny, Joe and Eddie Touhy the finer points of the criminal life. Weighing in at least 450 pounds, the Bear waddled when he walked. But he was a solid figure full of fighting vigor and brutal vitality. He was also an ignorant man, blatant and profane, utterly fearless when given to one of his choking rages.

The Bear's place was a dingy saloon at 14th Street and South Halstead. There was a sawdust floor "to soak up the blood" as Jack Lait said. A dirty, bent bar filled an entire wall. The rest of the room was packed with rickety tables and grimy wooden benches. On the drab smoke-stained walls hung pictures of John L. Sullivan, Jake Kilrain and dozens of other Irish fighters whom the Bear admired.

The Bear, whose specialty was making police records disappear, worked seven days a week. With a dirty apron tied around his enormous waist he held court, ruling over his kingdom with an iron fist like an absolute dictator. The Bear was feared by the killers that surrounded him, so much so that throughout his long career none dared to question him or usurp his authority.

During the Bear's leadership, no gang in all of Chicago was tougher or bolder. Every criminal in the Valley had to swear allegiance to Paddy the Bear or they didn't work in the Valley.

It came to be that the Bear's friend, Red Kruger, was sent to Joliet Penitentiary on a variety of charges. Soon afterward Runty Quinlan, the Bear's second in command, started sleeping with Kruger's wife.

This sordid romance threw the Bear into one of his rages. One day when the Runt stopped by Paddy's saloon for a beer, the Bear came from around the bar and called him every name in the book. He punched the Runt to the floor, picked him up and punched him to the floor again and again and again. It was a terrible beating, even by Valley standards. When it was over, the Bear told the Runt that he would beat him senseless every time he saw him.

Runty Quinlan swore his revenge.

Several days after the beating, Paddy the Bear was summoned to the Des Plains police station to answer a charge for receiving stolen property. "He could have," noted one cop, "found his way blind-folded."

It was morning when the Bear started out for the police station. He waddled along Blue Island Avenue and stopped by Eddie Tancel's place. Eddie was another Valley Gang graduate who operated a bar in the area. Once a professional fighter, Tancel—who was called "the Bulldog of Cicero"—had won almost all of his fights with his famous knockout punch. He retired to his Blue Island bar after he accidentally killed an up-and-coming fighter named Young Greenberg with his gloved fist. The police would eventually close down Tancel's Blue Island saloon after it became the scene of one too many shooting murders.

After leaving Tancel's place, the Bear crossed an alley just a half block from his saloon when Runty Quinlan sprang up from behind some trash cans and shot Paddy the Bear several times in his enormous belly. Paddy reeled out into the middle of the street, slumping down on the cobblestone and fell to the ground. Quinlan stood over the Bear and fired four more bullets into him.

Paddy the Bear was rushed to a hospital where a cop asked if he knew who had shot him. To which Paddy replied, "Of course I know who shot me, you idiot." Then he paused and said, more to himself than to anyone present, "But I didn't think that the little runt would have the nerve to do it."

Then he died.

For the cops, the Bear's last words were everything but a confession. Runty Quinlan was dragged in for questioning but was released due to lack of evidence.

Shortly after killing the Bear, Runty Quinlan went down state to Joliet State Prison on an unrelated charge. He was released several years later during Prohibition and opened a saloon on 17th and Lommis Streets at the border of the Valley. The place soon became a favorite hang-out for the Klondike and Myles O'Donnell boys. Once, when police raided the joint, they found ten bulletproof vests, two machine guns and a dozen automatic pistols hidden behind the bar. "The Runt's saloon," said Jack Lait "was that kind of joint."

Paddy the Bear had one son, known as "Paddy the Cub." Paddy the Cub idolized his father who, for all his wicked ways, was an indulgent and doting parent. Young Paddy never forgot his father's murder and for years nursed his hatred of Runty Quinlan. As a teenager he would see the Runt on his way to school, leaning against the doorway of his saloon, uneasily smiling down at him.

One day the Runt was lounging in a booth in

his saloon with three Valley Gang graduates: Fur Sammons, Klondike and Myles O'Donnell. The group had been drinking for several hours and were mildly drunk when Paddy the Cub slipped up to the Runt, jammed a revolver in his left temple and whispered "This is for my father, you son-of-a-bitch." He shot the Runt through the back of the head. After the Runt fell to the floor, Paddy the Cub fired several more shots into the body and then slowly and calmly walked out the front door of the saloon.

• • •

In 1919, after the Bear was killed, Terry Druggan and Frankie Lake took over the Valley Gang. Druggan was a dwarf-like little man with a hair-trigger temper and a lisp. He was ambitious and found the Valley territory too restrictive for his high ambition. He soon extended his criminal reach far beyond its borders.

Over the years, Terry Druggan had gained a reputation as a fool and a clown. Despite this reputation Druggan proved to be a highly effective leader. He was a smooth operator and a highly intelligent hood, and by the third year of Prohibition he had made himself and most of his gang members rich beyond their wildest dreams. By 1924, Terry Druggan could truthfully boast that even the lowest member of his gang wore silk shirts and had a chauffeur for his new Rolls-Royce.

Druggan was smart enough to enter into several lucrative business agreements with Johnny Torrio. He was wise enough to pull the Valley Gang off the streets and remodel them after Johnny Torrio's restructured version of "Big Jim" Colosimo's outfit. With his alcohol millions, Druggan bought a magnificent home on Lake Zurich and a winter estate in Florida. He surrounded himself with yes-men and flunkies and parked twelve new cars in his garage. He had a swimming pool although he couldn't swim, a tennis court although he didn't play, and dairy cattle (which he admitted scared him), sheep and swine in his pastures. He owned a thoroughbred racing stable and raced his horses, draped in his family's ancient Celtic color scheme, at Chicago's tracks.

Once, when he was ruled off the turf at one track for fixing a race, Druggan pulled his gun on the officials and promised to kill them all then and there if they didn't change their ruling. They changed their ruling.

Frankie Lake grew up with Druggan in the Valley. He and Druggan were inseparable companions, as well as business partners in everything. They even went to jail together.

In 1924, during the height of Prohibition, both Druggan and Lake were sentenced to a year in the Cook County jail by Judge James Wilkerson for contempt of court for refusing to answer questions regarding their business dealings. Lake appealed to the President of the United States for help. The President refused to intervene and the pair went to jail—sort of. After a $20,000 cash bribe to Sheriff Peter Hoffman, "for the usual considerations and conveniences" as Druggan put it, he and Lake were allowed to turn their cells into working offices. They came and went from the jail as they saw fit and were often seen in cafés late at night, retiring to their spacious apartments on ritzy Lake Shore Drive.

On those rare days when they actually stayed in the jail—waking up late and having breakfast in bed—their wives were regular visitors. In fact, on several occasions Druggan had his dentist brought in to fill a cavity. Later, when the story broke, a reporter asked Druggan to explain his absence from jail. The gangster explained, "Well you know, it's awfully crowded in there." He was right. In 1924 the Cook County jail, which had been built to house no more than 500 inmates, was home to over 1,500 men.

The same thing happened in 1933 when Druggan was supposed to be in Leavenworth Federal Prison for two and a half years on a tax evasion charge. Once again he bought his way out of the jail and was living in the tiny town just outside the prison, in a three bedroom apartment with his girlfriend Bernice Van De Hauten. She was a buxom blonde who moved down from Chicago to keep Terry company, much to his wife's surprise. The story broke and Druggan was moved from Leavenworth to Atlanta, without his girlfriend this time.

With the end of Prohibition, the Druggan and Lake Gang, as the Valley Gang was then called, was completely absorbed by the Chicago syndicate operations and for all practical purposes ceased to exist.

Roger Grows Up

As dyed-in-the-wool members of the old Valley Gang, the older Touhy boys learned the dark arts of burglary, daylight holdups and labor extortion, at which they excelled. There is a story that became underworld legend, how one stormy night in 1909, Patrolman James Touhy was walking his beat when he confronted his eldest son, Jimmy leaving Paddy the Bear's saloon with a burglar's bag over his shoulder. The normally quick-tempered Touhy remained uncharacteristically calm.

"Open the bag," his father said.

When the young man did as he was told, out rolled burglary tools and a bottle of nitroglycerin—an explosive used on difficult safes around the turn of the century. The elder Touhy cuffed his son and then called a paddy wagon to have the boy taken to the station to be booked.

"You book him," he told the cop behind the desk. "It's bad enough to arrest my own son without going to court to testify against him."

Nothing good came from the Touhy boys. In 1917 Jimmy Touhy was killed in a botched robbery attempt. His brother, Joe Touhy was killed in a freak shooting ten years later. Brother John tracked down Joe's killer and murdered him, only to die of consumption in the state prison several years later. Tommy Touhy, the second eldest and most fearless and feared of the lot, grew to be a ruthless outlaw who well deserved his nickname "Terrible Touhy." By 1919, Tommy was one of Chicago's leading hoods.

With poverty and crime on the rise in the Valley, James Touhy gave up on his elder sons, and, early in the summer of 1908, he moved his daughters, Eleanor and Eileen, and ten-year old son Roger to the tiny village of Downer's Grove. The village had been created only seventy-five years earlier, taking its name from a New Englander, Pierce Downer, who settled on what had been the crossing of two ancient Indian trails.

In Downer's Grove, Roger became a better-than-average baseball player and an above-average student. In general it was a pleasant time in his life. "It was a good enough boyhood," he remembered. "I played baseball and raised the usual amount of the devil and got teased because my hair was curley. [sic] If I had anything to gripe about, I didn't realize it, because the other boys didn't have any more than I did, generally speaking."

He took up ham operations as a hobby and built his own set at home and learned the international code. He attended St. Joseph's Roman Catholic church and school while the parish was still being run out of a hall over the top of the Des Plains hardware shop.

Since the family was strapped for cash, Roger worked around the parish as a handyman and assistant to the parish priest and its first pastor, Father Eneas Goodwin. Roger's duties included serving

28

mass as an altar boy and accompanying the priest as his driver in a rented horse buggy on his twice weekly rounds. "At whatever house we stopped there would be refreshments—apple pies, lemonade, thick sandwiches, salads, pickles, ice cream. Father waved the food away, but I ate fit to bust a gut....In the church there was a big oil painting of the Last Supper. Father Goodwin explained it to me, saying that a man called Judas had betrayed Jesus Christ for thirty pieces of silver. A thing like that can have a remarkable influence on a kid. I began thinking of Judas as a stool pigeon, a word I knew as did all youngsters. While sweeping up the church and dusting the pews I would stop and look for a long time at the painting. I picked out the face of a man I figured was Judas, and I would stand there hating him."

In 1915 Roger Touhy graduated from the eighth grade as class valedictorian and, as did many boys his age at that time, went job hunting and tried to land a position as an international wireless radio operator. However, his youth (he was only thirteen) kept him out of that line. Instead, he worked as an office boy and stock room clerk. He later took another position as a cookie taster in a biscuit bakery.

He was a determined adolescent and in 1915, the year his father retired from the Chicago police force, Roger lied about his age and managed to land a position with Western Union for twelve dollars a week. Of his age Touhy said, "...it was easy to get by. My hair was gray at the sides of my head (maybe I worried as an infant) before I got out of knee pants and every day I would have a five o'clock shadow by lunch time." He became the manager of a little residential section branch office and considered himself "a real big dealer."

Western Union taught Touhy the Morse code

which was easy enough since he already had experience. He was moved to a main office in midtown as an operator where he ran a book-making operation on the side. He even took the occasional bet from his father, of whom he said, "...[h]e liked to play the horses. He would bet fifty cents or one or two bucks on a race when he had the cash to spare. And now I was in a position to be his personal tout. The stable owners, trainers and jockey would send messages on the chances of their horses over the wires. I tipped off my father."

Touhy continues, "A really important thing happened to me—back then in 1915—was that a dark-haired Irish girl went to work for Western Union in the company branch office in Chicago's finest hotel— the Blackstone. She was fresh out of telegraph school. From the main office I sent the Blackstone's messages to her and received the ones she transmitted back. She sent better than she copied, but she wasn't good at either. I tried to help her."

' Her name was Clara Morgan. She was just sixteen and six years later Touhy would marry her. Clara worked the four-to-midnight shift, and since Touhy worked the day shift he would drop by to see her and eventually to walk her home. They were normally accompanied by one of Clara's co-workers, Emily Ivins who years later would be an instrumental witness to Touhy's innocence on kidnapping charges.

Sometime in 1916, Touhy became involved with the Commercial Telegraphers Union (C.T.U.) of America which was trying to organize the Western Union and Postal Telegraph Company. According to Touhy, during one of his breaks, he walked into the men's smoking lounge and read one of the union pamphlets that had been scattered across the room by organizers. Someone reported him to the management who called him in for interrogation. They asked Touhy if he was a union member, if he was acquainted with any union members and would he be willing to provide their names. Touhy said he wasn't a member, he didn't know any members and if he did he wouldn't give out their names. "So," one of the managers asked, "you intend to take a union card?"

Touhy replied "maybe" and was fired on the spot. "I should have lied to that superintendent," he wrote. "Honesty was my downfall."

That evening an organizer for the C.T.U. came to Touhy's house and told him that he was already blacklisted within the telegraph industry. Touhy didn't believe him and applied for work with the Associated Press which needed telegraph operators. They refused to take his application. He describes the incident saying, "I could have been a bearded Bolshevik with a bomb under my coat."

So he became a union organizer, probably the only job he could find in the only business he knew anything about.

One of the first things Touhy did was to forge the names of ten Western Union employee-informants on union application membership cards and give them to one of the secretaries in the union's office who Touhy suspected of being a plant.

Among the names he provided to her was the Western Union employee who had turned him in to management for reading union literature. The next day all of the people named on the fake application cards were fired and the secretary was terminated.

It was at this point that Touhy would meet some of the legends of labor organizing.

"Their faces" Roger wrote, "were scar tissued

31

from fighting hired strike breakers on picket lines. Their skulls were creased from bumping their heads on the tops of police paddy wagons. Their knuckles sometimes were driven halfway up to their wrists from past impacts."

One of the legends he met was Con Shea who was "an erudite character who delighted in using fancy words."

One evening over a beer he taught the young Touhy that "a divided septum is an occupational hazard of the profession of union organizing." Touhy said, "I nodded wisely not wanting to appear dumb. I learned later that he was talking about a busted nose."

Shea should have known about broken noses. He, along with "Big Frenchy" Mader, "Big Tim" Murphy and "Dapper" Dan McCarthy (a professional gunner later employed by Johnny Torrio) all but created the great Chicago Building Trades War of 1922. During the war—and it was a war by all definitions—Shea and the others worked both sides of the fence, for labor and for management, bombing both sides equally. The war ended when Big Frenchy Mader walked into the union hall with a machine gun and declared himself President and owner of the Building Trades Council. At that point there were so few people left that no one opposed him. Six years later, Shea's co-terrorist, Big Tim Murphy was gunned down during the violent Republican pineapple primary of 1928, so-called because of the throwing of bombs. By 1929, Shea, who had been a bomber for the Teamsters since he was sixteen, was now an old man taking any job he could find.

Roger soon tired of organizing; the hours were long, the pay was low and often the work was brutal

32

and dangerous. Except for a still-blossoming romance with Clara Morgan, Roger had nothing to hold him in Chicago, and, like thousands of young men before him, he headed out west to make his fortune. He left Chicago for St. Paul, but he was unable to find work. Touhy describes his plight, "[I was] dead broke. I bummed my way out of the city aboard a freight train."

Eventually, Roger found work as a telegraph operator for various railroads and commercial houses as he made his way out west. During his travels he worked as an operator for the Union Pacific Railroad, then as a telegraph operator and later as a brakeman on the Northwestern Railroad. Finally he accepted a position as a telegrapher for $185 a month on the Denver & Rio and Grand Railroad and was sent out west by the company, often to Colorado, with most of his time spent in Eagle County.

It was here in Eagle where he befriended Clyde Nottingham, who was said to be the meanest cowboy in the region if not in the state. A giant of a man with a short temper, Nottingham grew up in the rough and tumble world of mining camps. He was a man beset with endless personal problems, and he acted as the local bully. "When he wanted something," a relative noted, "he just took it."

In 1899, Clyde married Tillie Samuelson. They had three children, a daughter Lola and twin sons, Harold and Clyde Jr. Harold, who was said to have been a bright child, died at age two, after a week's illness, and Clyde Jr. died in infancy.

Clyde had moved to the area from Iowa at the age of seven. Like his father, teamster William Henry Nottingham, he was known to be mean to the bone. Both men were known to threaten with death anyone that dared cross them.

In 1904, Clyde Nottingham beat and threatened to kill a depot agent named H.G. Comstock and then ordered him out of town. A few days later the clerk spotted Nottingham walking toward him, pulled out a revolver and fired three shots. Comstock failed to kill him but did manage to cut a hole through his pants and give him flesh wounds in two other places. A trial was held, but the jury, knowing Nottingham's reputation, acquitted the depot agent, who left town that same day. A while later Nottingham was arrested for beating up another depot agent—the one Roger Touhy replaced.

Several days after arriving in town Roger Touhy—the five-foot four-inch, ninety-eight-pound kid from Chicago's Valley who never backed down— met Nottingham, the giant rancher with the quick fists.

Roger remembered Nottingham: "I got my first warning of western bad-man danger when a local merchant told me, 'You won't be here long, sonny, we got a rancher, Clyde Nottingham, who runs depot agents out of town. He carries a gun. Guess he don't like you depot agent dudes.'"

He continues, "It was cold that first night in Eagle and I had the stove red hot as I jiggled the telegraph key, handling the freight car, stock car and personnel messages. The waiting room door opened and in came a big man in cowboy clothes and a sheepskin coat. He spat on the potbellied stove.

"I walked to the ticket window, looked out and saw the caller was carrying a .45. He didn't look pleasant, but damned if he was going to run me out of town. 'Mr.,' I asked. He nodded and I said 'Mr. Nottingham anytime you want to spit on the stove go right ahead. But come back the next day after the stove cools and polish it. I ain't going to do it.'"

Remarkably an agreement was reached. Touhy agreed to put Nottingham's letters on the late train and in turn, Nottingham agreed to stop spitting in Touhy's fire. This was the beginning of what Touhy would deem "a fine friendship." Touhy was invited to spend time at Nottingham's ranch with his family. Touhy admits this gave him a "sense of belonging," which he appreciated.

Spending his free time at Nottingham's three-hundred-acre ranch, complete with stream, lake and seven bedroom house, Roger learned big game hunting and horseback riding. He became a better-than-average marksman and acquired his life-long obsession with fishing.

Roger left Eagle after a two-year stay, and in 1918 enlisted in the Navy and was eventually stationed at Harvard University where he worked as a wireless operator and taught officers the Morse code.

"The Navy," as Roger liked to point out, "gave grounds for me, a boy from the eighth grade to say honestly to cops, bootleggers, convicts, prison guards and interviewers, 'I've been to Harvard.'"

Opting for an early out with the Navy Reserve, Roger was back in Chicago by 1919, living with his father in suburban Franklin Park and dating Clara Morgan, having kept in touch with her through long letters from Colorado and later from Boston. There was talk of marriage, but Roger set off for the west again, landing in Drummund, Oklahoma where the oil business was in full boom and fortunes were being made overnight.

"I didn't know any more about the oil business then a mink knows about sex hygiene, but I could learn....The Sinclair Oil people, in a moment of laxity hired me as a scout. The experience I had in that line was confined to watching silent western movies in which army scouts killed Indians," says Tuohy.

Actually the position he filled was as a driver to the world famous geologist Dick Raymond who had been brought in to determine which wildcat wells were producing the most oil and from that, decide which land was worth leasing. "There was nothing," he wrote "against my buying leases that Raymond recommended."

Learning everything he could about the oil business from Raymond, Roger took $1,000 out of his savings and purchased a 150-acre site that Drummond recommended. Within a month, he resold the lease for a 200 percent profit. He repeated the process twenty times in one year. Of that time Touhy said, "[I] never lost on any of them...the money was good, but I was a guy who liked the city. And my mind was on the girl at the telegraph key in the Blackstone Hotel."

He returned to Chicago with $25,000, a respectable fortune in 1920, "and," he liked to point out, "it had taken me less than a year to earn it."

"Terrible Tommy"

Sometime around 1915 "Terrible Tommy" O'Connor brought Tommy Touhy, and his brothers, Johnny, Eddie and Joe into the fold of organized crime.

O'Connor was an interesting character. Both he and his brother, "Darling Dave" O'Connor, once studied for the priesthood in their native Ireland. Terrible Tommy ended up as a graduate of the Valley Gang. Many even say that he was the true leader of the gang before Druggan and Lake converted it into a Capone satellite.

The O'Connors were primarily burglars, and, like the Touhy brothers, ran a taxi service as their cover since it allowed them a legitimate reason for being in any neighborhood at any time of the day or night. It was the O'Connors who introduced Tommy and the older Touhy boys to their true love, nitroglycerin. The Touhy boys used nitro to blow safes while they were active criminals between 1900 and 1924.

O'Connor was also dubbed "Lucky Tommy" because he seemed to always get away. But Tommy's luck ended one muggy Chicago night, when he and others burgled the safe at the Illinois Central Station and in the process somebody shot and killed the night watchman, Dennis Tierney, an off-duty Chicago policemen.

Although O'Connor and a hood named Jimmy Howard escaped, one of O'Connor's men, Harry Emerson, was captured. Emerson informed the police that it was O'Connor who fired the fatal shot that killed young Officer Tierney. He offered to tell that story in court in exchange for consideration and the State's Attorney agreed.

On November 12, 1919, O'Connor was arrested on robbery charges and promptly offered to cut a deal with the police. He would finger Harry Emerson as the cop killer but the States Attorney turned down Tommy's offer. O'Connor, who had dozens of childhood friends on the force, heard about the deal that Emerson had cut and decided that Emerson had to die before he went to trial.

O'Connor offered $200 to a childhood friend named Jimmy Chjerin if Chjerin would take the money to a hood named "Big Joe" Moran as a down payment for the assassination of Harry Emerson. Chjerin refused the offer, telling O'Connor that he had promised his father he would go straight.

"The Peacock of the underworld," as the papers called Chjerin, was a tough guy with a long record which included a stint at Bidwell Prison. He got away with most of his minor crimes because the cops liked him, and because his father Dominick Chjerin was a municipal court bailiff and saw most of the beat cops several times a week. The Peacock's father tried to keep his son out of trouble but when that failed, he fixed the records for him or called in a favor from the cops to let his son walk away from a charge.

But the cops and judges were growing tired of looking the other way. Jimmy the Peacock, they said, was out of control. Then Jimmy impregnated his girlfriend. In an effort to do the right thing he married her. When their child was born Jimmy the Peacock swore to his father and wife and infant son that he would change his ways and go straight. This is why he turned down Tommy O'Connor's orders to take the murder money to Big Joe Moran. The only problem was that O'Connor didn't take disobedience in the ranks lightly. O'Connor was worried that the next time Jimmy the Peacock got into trouble he might tell the cops what O'Connor had asked him to do.

The Peacock didn't worry about it very much. The cops had O'Connor on a rock-solid charge of murder with an eyewitness.

Then, friends bailed out Terrible Tommy O'Connor.

On January 21, 1919, Jimmy Chjerin was sitting in the back seat of a stolen Model-T Ford with Tommy O'Connor. A Valley hood, Louie Miller, was sitting in the front seat. The three of them were laughing and joking when suddenly O'Connor stopped laughing, turned to Jimmy the Peacock and pumped three shots from an army service revolver into the young man's temple. Jimmy the Peacock died immediately. O'Connor barked at Miller to drive to Stickney, a town just south of Chicago and find an empty ditch where they would dump the body. Miller did as he was told.

Six months later Jimmy The Peacock's young widow turned on the gas in her coldwater flat, killing herself and her infant daughter and Jimmy the Peacock's father swore revenge against O'Connor. Using his own criminal connections, Jimmy's father had O'Connor's driver, Louie Miller, kidnapped from a Montrose Avenue saloon and brought to police headquarters where, after a beating, he swore that he had seen Tommy O'Connor gun down Jimmy the Peacock. Detectives picked up Tommy O'Connor and booked him for murder.

On January 8, 1921, acting on a tip from the *Chicago Tribune*, the police grabbed Louie Miller at his sister's home. He was wearing only underwear and was clinging to the edge of the second floor window when the police dragged him inside and hauled him downtown for another beating and more questioning. Again Miller gave a sworn statement that it was Tommy O'Connor who killed Jimmy the Peacock and once again the cops arrested O'Connor for Jimmy the Peacock's murder. This time they had him. But O'Connor was able to post the $45,000 bail, which was the largest bail ever required in Chicago at that time. O'Connor disappeared as soon as he was released.

On March 23, 1921 Detective Sergeant Patrick O'Neill got a tip that O'Connor was hiding out at the home of his brother-in-law, William Foley, at 6415 South Washtenaw Avenue. Five detectives circled the house and O'Neill called inside for Terrible Tommy to surrender. O'Connor burst through the door, guns blazing and yelled "Well, I'll get one of you anyway!"

Officer O'Neill was standing in the center of the yard and was taken off guard by the suddenness of the attack. O'Connor cut him down before he could point the pistol in his hand. Detectives Tom McShane, Joe Ronan and William Fenn started shooting the very second O'Connor raced out the door and assumed that they shot O'Neill by mistake. Badly rattled the detectives stood over O'Neill's body weeping "Joe! Joe! Oh God!"

O'Neill would lie in his own blood for fifteen minutes, twisting in agony before the ambulance arrived and rushed him to St. Bernard's hospital where he died. Meanwhile, Tommy O'Connor leaped over a fence at the rear of his sister's yard and ran down 63rd and Western where, at gunpoint he leaped into a checkered cab and was driven a mile before leaping out. He commandeered another car driven by William Condonn who drove O'Connor to Stickney where one of his men ran a saloon. There he was provided with clothes and food.

The search for O'Connor was one of the greatest manhunts in the history of the city. The search by an angry police force went on for days in the city and the suburbs, but the cops came up empty. Then a report arrived that O'Connor had been seen at the Crystal Palace dance hall on the far south side. Cops raided the place while O'Connor was dancing the shimmy with some girls.

"Throw 'em up, Tommy!" the cops shouted.

There was chaos. The hall emptied quickly, some of the dancers were pressed against the wall and searched but O'Connor once again slipped away to freedom. It was rumored that O'Connor was dressed in women's clothes so as to make an easy escape.

The cops finally caught up with O'Connor on July 25, 1921. He was arrested with a Valley hood named Jimmy Gallagher in Minneapolis after an unsuccessful attempt at robbing a Pullman car on the Chicago Great Western passenger train bound for Omaha. As an extra embarrassment, the most wanted man in America was captured by a switch operator named W.L. Woods who was only armed with a hammer at the time.

A squad of heavily armed detectives was sent to St. Paul to bring O'Connor back to Chicago. It was an illegal transport, but since O'Connor was a two-time cop killer, no policeman in Chicago or St. Paul really cared about his civil rights. However, the state of Minnesota was charging O'Connor with an earlier payroll robbery and wanted him to stay in their state to stand charges. But the Chicago cops took O'Connor out of the city with such speed that the City Attorney, Floyd Olson, formally charged the Chicago Chief of Detectives with kidnapping. He sent three carloads of his detectives to bring O'Connor back but they were turned away at the city border.

On the way back to Illinois, O'Connor told the cops "It wasn't my revolver that killed him. He [Officer O'Neill] was shot down by his own pals. It was a mistake of course, but they shot him and after that mistake they ran away and put the blame on me. Do you wonder why I ran away? What chance did I have with every policeman in the city out to get me dead or alive? Me, the con, only a hundred and thirty-eight pounds? I never shot anybody, at least not to kill, in my life."

He said the same thing in court but nobody was listening then either. On September 24, 1921, O'Connor was found guilty of first degree murder and was sentenced to be hanged. The date of execution was set for December 15, 1921. When the judge read the verdict, there was a cry from O'Connor's father who was sitting with his other son, Darling Dave. Since his time working as a hood with Tommy, "Darling Dave" O'Connor had become a LaSalle Street investment broker. However, he lost his license for immoral conduct in 1919. "It's the wrongest [sic] verdict in the world," he told reporters about his brother's sentence, "we couldn't get justice, we couldn't get justice."

On October 15, 1921, Judge Kickham Scanlan denied O'Connor a new trial and the decision and the death sentence stayed. O'Connor was ordered to be held in the criminal courts building until his hanging. From his cell there, he could hear the scaffolding of the hangman's platform being built.

On December 15, 1921, a man was seen driving his car to a street outside of the criminal courts building where O'Connor was being held. The man parked and then walked up and down the street outside the jail and then tossed a package into an open window. Most believe it was the guns O'Connor would use to escape that day.

O'Connor may not have needed the guns since it's commonly agreed that either he bribed his way out of his death cell or was simply let free by guards; one way or the other, his daring daylight escape was spectacular.

Tommy Touhy, who hung out with Darling Dave O'Connor at a saloon on Hoyne and Madison Streets in the Valley, boasted openly about providing the two guns for Tommy O'Connor's fabulous escape from prison. He even claimed that he had engineered the entire incident. However, another story was that the guns were smuggled into the jail by way of a pork chop sandwich. The guns were intended for another prisoner, but the jail's cook, William Fogarty, a convict himself, gave the weapons to Tommy's cellmate, a man named Charles McDermott.

Since it was a Sunday the prisoners were allowed to walk in the yard for their exercise. The guard on duty in the yard was David Strause who later reported that LaPorte and O'Connor stood up close to him while O'Connor said he was ill and needed a pass to the hospital.

When the guard bent over to write the pass, Laporte and O'Connor jumped him from behind and then O'Connor whipped out a pistol and stuck it into the guard's ribs while Darrow took his keys.

The other prisoners in the yard saw the escape and crowded around but O'Connor turned his gun on them and ordered them back into their cell blocks. Then, O'Connor and his four men ran down the stairs and overpowered guards Charles Moore, Thomas Jefferson and Thomas Wetta. They were all bound and gagged but not before Wetta managed to yell out, "Prisoner escaping!" alerting the other guards on duty.

On the run now, the prisoners scaled a wall by jumping on a shed and then over the 9-foot wall. Laporte, a heavy set man, broke both of his ankles as he fell and was quickly recaptured.

Darrow and McDermott fled in a different direction than O'Connor. They were recaptured by the police within a half hour. O'Connor escaped by leaping onto a passing car's running board. As he jumped, the clerk of the jail, Austin Jacobson, grabbed his coattail but let go when O'Connor spun around and pointed the gun at him. After the car turned the corner Tommy O'Connor was gone.

When questioned by police about the escape, Dave O'Connor, Tommy's father said "We knew the power of God would save Tommy and show the police and all the people that were against him that he was innocent. We're going to have a merry Christmas at our home now."

On December 17, 1921, the body of a man was found under a bridge three miles north of Palmyra, Wisconsin in rural Jefferson County. He had been shot with a .32-caliber revolver. The police theorized that O'Connor had forced his way into the man's car and then made him drive out across the state line. There, O'Connor found it more expedient to kill the man rather than face a kidnapping charge. The body was stripped of its clothes and wallet and left face down in the mud.

Then a note arrived from Milwaukee in Tommy O'Connor's hand "Chief: Don't send anybody after me. I am innocent. Much obliged to Struass. I am gone but my friends will reward him/Good luck to you all. I will be posted by friends and will shoot the first man who comes near me."

The Chicago police assumed O'Connor had hidden out in St. Paul and then slipped over the Canadian boarder before traveling to Ireland. However the last place that Tommy O'Connor was seen alive was in that tiny village of Elkhorn, Wisconsin, on December 10, 1922.

The Bootlegger

When Roger Touhy returned to the Valley he invested most of his small fortune into a used car dealership not far from the tiny house in the Valley where he was born.

"My automobile business," Touhy said, "was bringing me in from $50,000 to $60,000 a year. But the big money was in alcoholic beverages. Everybody in the racket was getting rich. How could the bootleggers miss, with a short ounce of gagging moonshine selling for $1.25, or an eight-ounce glass of nauseating beer going for 75 cents?"

The Touhy brothers, Johnny, Eddie, Tommy and Joe had already gotten involved in the booming bootleg business via Terrible Tommy O'Connor. They worked mostly as hired enforcers, but they occasionally hijacked a syndicate beer truck. It was almost natural that Roger join them and eventually he entered the bootlegging business. They entered the business through the back door, leasing a small fleet of trucks with drivers, from syndicate boss Johnny Torrio's enormous bootlegging operation. Using the money they earned from those leases, Roger and his brothers bought a franchise from Torrio for the beer delivery routes to rural northwestern Cook County, the area where Roger grew up.

The beer delivery business could be lucrative as long as expenses were kept to a minimum, so the notoriously tight-fisted brothers opted not to pay for police protection. As a result, Chicago and Cook County police, probably working in a 50/50 split with Johnny Torrio, or at the least working under his orders, made a practice of stopping and impounding the brothers' trucks, probably kicking back half the fines collected to Torrio.

When the expenses started to mount it occurred to Tommy Touhy that the police would never suspect a commercial vehicle of delivering booze. They decided to test the theory. The boys bought two used Esso Gasoline trucks—Esso being the forerunner to Exxon—and they made several successful shipments that way. It was a practice they continued to use even though most of the drivers the Touhys employed were off-duty cops. Virtually every truck the Touhys owned was disguised as a meat delivery truck. After that, their trucks were never stopped and the brothers shipped all their beer in commercial vehicles, either marked as gasoline, meat or coal delivery trucks.

Ambitious and flush with cash from the beer routes, the brothers entered a bootlegging partnership with two north side Chicago hoods, Willie Heeney and Rocco DeGrazio, both of whom were amateur narcotics dealers who would eventually reach top spots in the syndicate under Frank Nitti and Tony Accardo. The Touhys and their new partners pumped out rot-gut beer from a rented garage and made enough money to open a short-lived nightclub a few doors down from their brewery. Using their profits from the brewery and speakeasy, Roger and Tommy opened a string of handbooks, and then used the cash from that to buy Heeney and DeGrazio out of the business.

Now the prosperous owner of a beer delivery service, a small brewery, several handbooks and a car dealership, Roger asked Clara Morgan for her hand in marriage. She accepted and the couple married in a simple church ceremony in Chicago on April 22, 1922.

For the next three years, the brothers worked to develop their various enterprises, building up their suburban beer routes and expanding into labor extortion and gambling, but like most other Irish hoods, resisting the easy money of prostitution. Then, in late 1925, as Johnny Torrio was just beginning to expand his criminal empire, the brothers leaped out of the small time by entering a partnership with Matt Kolb, a five-foot three-inch, 280 pound former ward politician, syndicate bagman and pay-off expert, who ran a $3,000,000 rot-gut whisky and needle beer brewery not far from Roger's car dealership.

Earlier in the year Al Capone, who was then still Johnny Torrio's chief of staff, told Kolb that he was out of business unless he paid 50 percent of his gross to Rocco DeGrazio, Roger's former business partner and Capone's new business agent on the north side. Although Kolb acted as bagman for Johnny Torrio, he despised Capone. Rather than work for him, Kolb called Roger and Tommy Touhy and by mid-year their partnership was in place. It was a simple arrangement: Kolb was the money man, Roger was business manager and Tommy was the muscle.

It was Kolb who encouraged Touhy to move his operation out to the suburbs, largely because his brothers were already operating in the area and because Kolb understood that peace would never reign in Chicago as long as prohibition was in force. But Kolb also held considerable clout with the new County Sheriff, Charles Graydon, who had owned an ice packing business several years before. The brothers knew Kolb was right: peace would never reign in Chicago's underworld with so many different—and violent—street gangs vying for a limited amount of business. But that wasn't the case out in the rural northern portion of the county. In fact, when the brothers first started peddling the syndicate's beer they were stunned at the amount of business, both existing and potential, that was out there. Better yet, there was barely any competition for the market and there were scores of people willing to operate speakeasies if Kolb, who was worth a million in cash, put up the money to open them.

By 1926, the Touhy brothers and Matt Kolb were operational in suburban Des Plains, a small but prosperous community where they started a cooper shop, brewery and wort plant. They expanded that to ten fermenting plants, working round the clock, each plant being a small brewery in itself with its own refrigeration system and ice-making machine with a bottling plant. The investment paid off. By the end of the year, the partners were selling 1,000 barrels of beer a week at $55 a barrel with a production cost of $4.50 a barrel.

They sold their beer to 200 roadhouses outside of Chicago, mostly in far western Cook and Will County, north to the Wisconsin Lake region. Richer then ever, they hired more muscle men and with Tommy Touhy leading the assault, the brothers punched, shot and sold their way into a considerable portion of the upper northwest region of the city, "Our business"

Roger said, "was scattered over a lot of mileage. A barrel here and a barrel there. Nobody realized that Matt and I were grossing about $1,000,000 a year from beer alone....I didn't become a giant in the racket, but you might say I was one of the biggest midgets who ever scoffed at the Volstead law."

Since making wort—the main ingredient for beer as well as bread—was legal, Roger and Kolb claimed their entire operation was a bakery since "I was producing enough wort for all the bread baked in a dozen states. It was a big enterprise and I paid fifteen cents tax on every gallon I made."

To counter Chicago's off-beer season—the winter months—they set up a slot machine business, placing 225 machines in gas stations, dance halls and chicken dinner stands. "The only way to make money faster" he said, "is to have a license to counterfeit bills."

They kept the local politicians happy, aside from bribing them outright, by doling out 18,000 free bottles of beer every week through one of Kolb's underlings, Joe Goebel of Morton Grove. The County President, Anton Cermak not only took the beer which he resold or gave away to the party faithful, but had Touhy print his name and picture on the front label.

To keep the cost of police protection low, always a priority with the Touhys, they hired off-duty Cook County highway patrolmen. "Our local law," Roger wrote, "was mostly Cook County Highway Patrol. I figured out a way to keep the roads open for us, with top priority for our beer trucks. Whenever we had a job open as a truck driver or what not, I hired a cop right away from the highway patrol to fill it...we paid no man less than $100 a week, which was more than triple what the patrol guys got for longer hours."

In as far as the Touhy gang went, at least before 1927, there really wasn't any gang, not in the traditional sense. Rather, the entire operation was run more along the lines of any other prospering suburban-based business. Jim Wagner, Touhy's bookkeeper, told the FBI that the Touhy gang had an average of twenty to twenty-five members before the war with Capone, that the gang had no official headquarters only an after work hangout, an old gas station "in back of Mrs. Kolze's white house in Shiller Park."

Another hangout was Wilson's Ford dealership in Des Plains run by Henry Ture Wilson, who, according to the FBI, not only sold most of the Touhy gang discounted Fords, but also dealt in stolen cars. Wilson's stockroom manager, Otto Rexes, ran a handbook for Roger out of the place as well. Roger also purchased most of his beer delivery trucks here under his garage's name, the Davis Cartage Company. On most Saturday nights gang members could be found at the Dietz Stables, a dance hall in Ivanhoe in Lake County.

After the war with Capone started, the gang leaped in size to about fifty men who worked for Touhy on a regular basis, according to Jim Wagner, one of the first men to work with Touhy when he moved out to Des Plains.

George Wilke, who was also known as George Fogarty, had been one of Touhy's minor partners in the beer business for three years but left it, "because living in the country gave me enough sinus troubles to have to move to Florida."

Walter Murray, forty-two, was a truck driver and laborer in the organization. Murray wore false upper teeth, yet all of the lower teeth were missing except for the two front ones. Like most of the men who worked for Touhy, Murray was from the Valley and had a wife and four children and no criminal record.

Jimmy Clarence Wagner, forty, worked as Touhy's bookkeeper, although he and his brother John ran a small painting business out of Elmwood Park. Married in 1918 and with a ten-year-old son, James Jr., the family lived in Chicago until 1926 before finally moving out to Des Plains. Wagner had enlisted in the army during the first war and served as a sergeant in the artillery corps. After his discharge from the service he worked for Edison Kees as a flooring salesman until 1920 when he became involved with the city employees' annuity fund as a clerk for three years. He then went to work for his brother-in-law Leonard Thompson who knew Matt Kolb. Kolb introduced him to Touhy, who in 1930 hired him as a truck driver at $50.00 a week. Soon he was promoted to collector. He never used "muscle," never carried a gun and always had friendly dealings with his customers.

Willie Ford was a collector who lived in Des Plains for four years, leaving in 1929 and then returning after the shooting war with the DeGrazios had started. His brother, Jerry Ford, was a truck driver living on 4th Street in Des Plains. Willie Ford later became Touhy's chief enforcer and strong-arm man. Ford's roommate was Arthur Reese, a gang regular and enforcer. Other enforcers included Jim Ryan who was, at least on paper, the foreman in charge of the drivers and lived on Grand Avenue in River Forrest. His brother, Clifford Ryan, lived across the street from the Des Plains elementary school. Working under Ryan were enforcers John (Shaner) Crawford and Joseph (Sonny) Kerwin.

John "Red" Ryan, one of Paddy the Bear's sons,

had worked for the Shelton gang for a while and was a member of the gang along with Martin O'Leary and Old Harv Baily who were associated with the Touhy gang on a regular basis. Roy Marshalk said Wagner "was not a collector or a driver. He always rode with Touhy everywhere." Like everyone else, Ford was reluctant to discuss the dangerous Marshalk who was actually, after Tommy Touhy, the gang's chief of staff and high executioner.

Most of the bodyguards were former Cook County Highway patrolmen like Buck Henrichsen who also worked as a laborer and was known as a "muscle man." Henrichsen brought in his younger brother called "Buck Jr." and a second highway patrolman, Mike Miller, who acted as Tommy Touhy's personal bodyguard. Other bodyguards included August John La Mar and Louis Finko, two very dangerous men, as well as Roger's childhood friend Willie Sharkey and for a brief period, Gus Schafer who in 1930 was new to the area.

In 1933, Touhy's bodyguard Willie Sharkey said, "We always carried guns on beer runs to protect ourselves and friends from the syndicate, after 1930 we seldom left the north side and the vicinity of Des Plaines and very seldom went into Chicago or else we would have been placed on the spot. But we left town right after any of the newspapers pinned us with a crime. Tommy (Touhy) took care of that."

Although they may not have had a headquarters, the Touhy gang did have their own priest, Father Joseph Weber, who Roger had met back in 1923 when Weber was an Indiana State Prison chaplain while Tommy Touhy was serving time for his role in an Indianapolis department store burglary. Roger and his brother Eddie asked Weber to use his influence to get a parole hearing for Tommy. Weber agreed, and by the end of the year Tommy was paroled and the Touhys were indebted to a priest who ran one of the poorest parishes in Indianapolis. Later, after the brothers were established in the bootlegging business, they donated 10 percent of their business profits to Weber's parish. "I was," said Roger, "God's bagman."

The brothers benefitted the priest in other ways. Weber had always been politically active in Indianapolis and argued vehemently for the city's growing black population. Weber claimed that the Klu Klux Klan, which had its regional headquarters in Indianapolis, included some of the city's and state's leading families and politicians. As a result, Weber said, the black citizens of Indianapolis were denied even the most basic of city services.

One day as a passing part of a conversation, Weber mentioned to Tommy Touhy that if he had the Klan's secret membership files, he could confirm his suspicions and break their power. A few days later, on April 1, 1923, a moonlit Easter Sunday, a burglar broke into the Klan's headquarters and stole the organization's state membership list, some 12,208 names, which included some of the most powerful and well respected people in the Midwest. The next day, parts of the list were published in the Catholic newspaper *Tolerance* under the headlines "Who's Who in Indianapolis."

"The Klan offered me $25,000 for the records, which I turned down," Roger wrote.

Weber didn't always stay above the fray himself. John Sambo was a small time beer hall operator who managed Sambo's Place, a Capone saloon next to the Big Oaks Golf Course on the extreme northwest edge of Chicago. The problem was that the place bordered on Roger Touhy's territory. Tommy

Touhy paid Sambo a visit and he changed to Touhy's brand.

Sambo reported to the FBI that one sunny afternoon, Roger Touhy and several of his men, including Father Weber, entered the saloon at mid-day and drank until the sun went down. That night a young Negro boy came into the bar room to shine shoes and the drunken Touhys pulled out their weapons and fired shots at the boy's feet to make him dance.

Several months later, Sambo fell out of favor with the Touhys when he stopped selling their beer and switched to Capone's brand. An FBI report on Sambo states, "[On] one occasion Roger Touhy, George Wilke and Leroy Marshalk came into his place of business and took him down to the basement, stating that they had information that he was selling other beer. Sambo stated at that time that he believed that Touhy would have killed him, but that Marshalk, whom Sambo had known for some time, stopped him."

To the newspapers, the public, the police and the politicians, Roger's Des Plains operation looked exactly the way he and Kolb wanted it to look; like a hick, two-bit operation that grossed a few hundred thousand dollars a year. "And Touhy," Ray Brennan said, "was careful to foster that illusion. He lived well, but not lavishly in Des Plaines as it was a quiet town where he was considered a leading citizen. He was a contributor to charities and a member of fraternal organizations and golf clubs. Touhy and Kolb had a million-dollar-a-year business going plus a neat income from slot machines and a few road houses but they were wary enough not to brag about it. They were smart enough to pay income taxes on it."

Roger, who was now the father of two boys, made his final move to the suburbs in the spring of 1926 and purchased a large, comfortable home, just north of the center of Des Plains. His neighbors considered the bootlegger and his family respectable, hard-working people. "Nice," recalled one neighbor. "Not what you would think for a bootlegger. They were quiet people...refined."

"There was no stigma to selling beer." Touhy wrote. "I bought a place that some of the newspapers later called a 'mansion' or a 'gang fortress.' It was a six-room bungalow and later I put a sixty-foot swimming pool in the back. The only gang I ever had around there was a guard with a shotgun after the Capone mob tried to kidnap my kids....I lived quietly with my family during those big money years. I put a workshop, office and bar in my basement. There was a playhouse for the kids in my backyard. My wife got along well with our neighbors."

Even when Tommy and Roger were being hounded by the police during the John Factor kidnapping, their neighbors supported them. Des Plains historian Mark Henkes wrote, "Touhy gave his money freely to people and families in a pinch. He left baskets of food on the doorsteps of homes with a $20 bill attached to the basket handle. The recipients sometimes never knew where the food came from. He paid medical bills for some families. He made good money selling beer and he gave some of it away."

Even though Roger did his best to fit in, there were occasional setbacks like the incident when the *Chicago Tribune* and other groups were planning a historical pageant for Des Plains in which citizens would dress as early settlers and travel down the Des Plains river in wooden canoes. Meanwhile, Touhy wanted to get rid of some mash, the fermentation of beer, by pumping it into the river. He hired a crew to dig a trench and lay a sewer line from his plant to the river.

He poured hundreds, perhaps thousands of gallons of the mash into the river. The problem was that Des Plains was going through a dry season and the river was low and barely moving. The stench from the mash was unbearable. Father Patrick O'Connor, head of St. Mary's Training School in Des Plains and a member of the parade committee, got a whiff of the foul smell in the river and immediately knew what happened. O'Connor knew Roger and called him about the problem he had created. "What in the hell were you thinking, Rog? Half of Chicago will be here in a day and you turn the river into a flood of bootleg booze! Do something before the pageant starts."

Roger apologized and hired more then twenty boys from Maine High School in Des Plains to dump thousands of gallons of perfume into the river, "and the pageant was a sweet-smelling success."

So, while the public, the press and the police may have been fooled by Roger's small time image, Al Capone knew exactly how much money Touhy and Kolb were earning out on the dusty back roads of Cook County. He wanted a piece of it, a large piece of it. As he always did, Capone first tried to talk his way into a partnership explaining the benefits of working within his operation. They met a total of six times that year, in Florida, during the winter months on fishing trips, and Capone offered to let Roger use his yacht.

Touhy said, "He offered to let me use his yacht or stay in his big house, surrounded by a wall about as thick as Statesville's (prison) on Palm Island in Biscayne Bay between Miami and Miami Beach. I didn't accept."

Roger wrote that he had two business deals with Capone in 1927 because Capone had trouble getting beer for his joints. Capone called Touhy and asked him to sell him 500 barrels and since Touhy had a surplus he agreed and told Capone to send 500 empties to the cooperage. He would send 500 barrels back for the price of $37.50 per barrel, a discount because of the large order.

Capone called back and asked for another 300 barrels. Touhy agreed and told Capone when he expected to be paid. The day before the money was due, Capone called and said that 50 of the barrels were leakers and that he wouldn't pay.

"I'll pay you for seven hundred and fifty, ok?"

"You owe me for eight hundred and I expect to be paid for eight hundred."

"Well the boys told me there were some leakers, but I'll check on it."

Capone paid the $30,000 in cash and called a week later and asked for more. Touhy refused, saying his regular customers were taking all of his output. Knowing that it may have been Capone testing his ability to draw him in or to see what he could produce by taking him to be his biggest customer, "What was the use of needling him by saying I didn't do business with weasels."

In late 1927, Capone told Willie Heeney, Roger's former business partner, to go out to Des Plains to see Roger and encourage him to come around to Capone's way of thinking. By now, Heeney was working full time in the outfit's enormous prostitution racket where he would stay until the depression set in and he switched over to labor racketeering and narcotics. He soon became his own best customer and became hooked on heroin.

Roger agreed to meet Heeney at the Arch, one of

his road houses in Schiller Park, managed by his brother Eddie. Arriving with Heeney at the meeting was Frankie Rio, Capone's favorite bodyguard and enforcer whose presence was no doubt meant to impress Touhy. Heeney was the spokesman, telling them that Capone wanted to open the county for brothels, taxi dance halls and punch board rackets. He was willing to split the proceeds evenly with Kolb and Touhy to which Rio added, "Al says this is virgin territory for whorehouses."

Roger told Henney that he didn't want or need Capone as a partner, and that although the locals might tolerate speakeasies and gambling dens, whorehouses and taxi dance halls were something else. However, there was at least one brothel in operation in Des Plains at 304 Center Street, apartment 38, above Matt Kolb's brother's laundry store/handbook operation. There were at least three women working on the property and photos of the nude women were later taken from Willie Sharkey when he was arrested in Wisconsin. The FBI later noted that "there were many noisy parties in this apartment and numerous men visited them." A neighbor noted that "six men at a time would enter or leave the apartment together. The next group would enter the apartment only after the first group had left."

FBI agents later tracked down two of the women and described them in their reports as "nice looking women" and "very attractive women."

Among those identified as regulars to the apartment were "Chicken" McFadden, Basil Banghart and George Wilke. Willie Sharkey, Touhy's enforcer, rented an apartment in the building under the name T.J. Burns and used the Park Ridge Chief of Police as his reference.

Next, Capone sent Jimmy Fawcett and Murray "the Camel" Humpreys out to Des Plains to talk to Roger. The probable reason for sending Fawcett and Humpreys to see Touhy was, in all likelihood, to try one last time to get him to fall into line before the real shooting started. Sending Fawcett, an old hand Capone gunman, was a smart move. Touhy had known Fawcett for years, the two of them living along the edges of Chicago unionism for several years. Humpreys may have been new to Touhy. The Camel, Touhy said, did all the talking. Humpreys got things off to a bad start. He said Touhy was "putting [his] nose where it don't belong and that means trouble."

"Mr. Capone" the Camel hissed, "is upset at the Touhys and that isn't good." Capone wanted Touhy to stop offering protection to the Teamster Union bosses.

Afterward Roger went to Cicero with him and Fawcett and talked over the problems with Frank Nitti. There are several versions of what happened next, but the end result of each version is the same.

When the Camel was done with his threats, Touhy put a pistol into his mouth and told him never to show his face in Des Plains again. Humpreys offered to buy back his life with his new car but Touhy let them go. After the pair had left, Fawcett returned and offered "to kill Humpreys on the way back into Chicago and for an extra few grand, Rog, I'll knock off that son of a bitch Nitti too."

Years later, Touhy told the story, or at least a cleaned up version of it, in his memoir. When the book hit the streets, an infuriated and humiliated Murray Humpreys denied that it ever happened.

Capone tried a different tactic; he would push Touhy to see how far he could get before a shooting war broke out. Starting in the early summer of 1927, he tried to work his way into Touhy's territory by opening several whorehouses just inside Des Plains. That same day, Roger and Tommy Touhy, backed by several truckloads of their men and a squad of Cook County police, raided the bordellos, broke them up and chased the women back to Chicago. All the while, Capone kept sending his beer salesmen into Touhy's territory where they achieved a fair amount of success by drastically undercutting Touhy's prices, but the ever shrewd Kolb recognized Capone's ploy and refused to be prodded into a price war that they couldn't win. Instead, the Touhys responded by sending a simple message to any saloon keeper who sold Capone's beer inside their territory. If the bar owner sold Capone's brew, they would wreck the place. If he continued, they would burn his place to the ground. That was the way Joe Touhy, Roger's older brother, died, in June of 1929. Eyewitnesses said that Joe and his crew were breaking up a speakeasy that the Capones had opened in Schiller Park. When a waiter reached for something under the bar, Joe Touhy's own man, a hood named Paul Pagen, fired off a warning burst from his machine gun, accidentally killing Touhy.

Johnny Touhy, the third eldest brother, didn't call it an accident. He killed Pagen in revenge for Joe's murder and was sentenced to prison for ten years to life. However he was released in four years, his brothers having purchased his freedom with bribes. "And that's what money," wrote the *Chicago Tribune* of John's release, "well spent in Chicago will do."

A few months after his parole was granted, Johnny was arrested again for attempted murder of a Capone goon. He was sent back to Stateville

Prison where he died of consumption in a barren hospital room.

The remaining brothers, Roger, Tommy and Eddie, declared war on Capone after Joe was killed and Johnny was jailed. From 1928 until 1930, the dusty back roads of northern Cook County ran red with gangster blood from an otherwise quiet gang war that went largely unnoticed until 1931, when all hell broke loose.

WAR

"It was a war, chiefly, between the Irish and the Italians. I'm Irish and I'd come into my office in the morning after another shoot-out and I would say to my co-worker, who was Italian, 'Well that's one to my side' and the next day he would come and say 'well, it's leveled Jim, we chalked one up on our side last night.' It was awful really, they were all such young men."

—James Doherty, crime reporter
for the *Chicago Tribune*

By 1930, Roger Touhy and Matt Kolb were millionaires. Their small, but profitable beer and gambling empire stretched from midtown Chicago to as far north as St. Paul, Minnesota. They owned dozens of speakeasies, roadside casinos, handbook parlors, three large breweries, and an enormous fleet of trucks. Roger saw repeal approaching and invested his earnings in a dry cleaning business with Kolb's brother, commercial real estate, a well digging company and a winter place for himself

in Florida. Unlike Matt Kolb or even his own brothers, Roger intended to be completely legitimate by
1933. Then he and Clara and their boys would sell
everything and move west to Colorado, although
Clara was holding out for Florida.

However, if Touhy was ready for prohibition to
end, the mob wasn't. The depression hurt more and
more of the mob's traditional enterprises like prostitution and gambling. Al Capone decided to take over
Chicago's labor racket business and gain control of
the Teamsters International strike fund, worth an
estimated $150,000,000 with another $10,000,000 a
year flowing into its coffers from membership dues.

Leading Capone's assault was George "Red"
Barker, a west side Irishman and former bookkeeper. Working under Barker as his assistant was the
up and coming Murray Humpreys, a Welshman who
had strong-armed his way into at least twenty-six
Teamster locals by then. When the decade of the
1930s opened, George Red Barker was, as one
Chicago cop put it, "riding on top of the world."
Barker all but controlled the Chicago Teamsters and
was reported to be earning $200,000 a year as a
result.

Before he took to a life of crime, Barker had been
an honest bookkeeper. He was literate, devouring
every union newsletter and newspaper he could find
from anywhere in the country, and paid for information on locals as well. Barker would get a copy of the
financials and study them. If the union had potential, Barker recommended the takeover to Ralph
Capone and Frank Nitti who talked it over with Al
Capone. If Capone agreed—and he almost always
did—Barker and his boys would go after the union.

In early 1931, Capone urged Barker to go after
the coal teamsters.

Barker approached James "Lefty" Lynch, a semi-honest thug who owned the Coal Teamsters Local 704, which delivered fuel to the entire downtown district where every office building depended upon the local for fuel to warm its buildings against the brutal Chicago winters. Barker told Lynch that Capone expected him to turn over half of the control of his union as well as his seat on the prestigious and important Joint Teamsters Council. In exchange, Barker offered Lynch protection. On the up side, Barker told Lynch, Capone intended to double the union's membership and as a result Lynch's income would double as well.

Lynch sat through Barker's speech and then threw him out of his office. It was his union and he wasn't going to give it up to Capone or anyone else.

Capone waited.

Later in the month, Lynch went to his summer home on Brown Lake outside Burlington, Wisconsin. His family was preparing a barbecue and the members were seated around a long picnic table when Danny Stanton and Klondike O'Donnell, two of the meanest Capone hoods in Chicago, drove into the yard. They climbed out of the car slowly. They were in no hurry. There were no cops or witnesses around for miles. They were armed with shotguns, pistols and rifles. Stanton walked over to Lynch and said, "The Big Fellow back in Chicago sends this message: you just retired from Local 704. From this moment on, you stay away from the union hall. You stay away from the office. You stay away from the Joint Council. You understand?"

Lynch nodded his head and Klondike added, "Well just so's you don't forget what was said...." and pulled out his pistol and shot Lynch through both of his legs while his wife and children looked on in horror. Lynch fell to the ground, groaning in agony. Stanton bent over Lynch to make sure he was alive and said "You got balls; I'll give you that." He stood up and turned to Lynch's daughter and said "get him to a doctor and he'll be alright."

At the next meeting of the Joint Council, Red Barker and Murray Humpreys appeared at the door with a dozen heavily armed Capone men.

Barker, carrying a baseball bat, stood in the center of the room and asked "Which one is Lefty Lynch's chair?" Somebody pointed to a large leather chair in the middle of the room and Barker sat there. He looked around the room and announced that he was now running the Coal Teamsters Chauffeurs and Helpers Union Local 704 and that everything would remain just the way Lynch had left it. The only difference was that the entire treasury was turned over to Capone except for $1,000 which was left to cover administrative payrolls.

After that, Barker went to the fuel dealers in the district and informed them that they were only hiring union members and that they were giving all of their drivers a massive pay raise or else Capone would see to it that not a lump of coal was delivered downtown.

The dealers had no choice but to agree and passed the cost along to the real estate developers who consequently raised the price of office space in the area. Capone kept Lynch on the payroll to avoid a revolt in the ranks. However, Lynch never appeared at another union function.

As a reward, Capone gave Barker control over the ushers' union with orders to exploit it to its full potential. Barker sent word to every theater owner in the city that they were to use his ushers for every political and sporting event, indoor or outdoor. He said they would have to pay for "crowd control," a service only his union could provide, at a rate of $10 per usher.

Movie theaters avoided the hike by paying off Barker in cash. Five dollars per usher was less expensive for them. Within weeks Barker was being paid off by every strip show, opera, ballet, symphony, prize fight and ball game held in the city. He was collecting a fortune until one prize fight promoter named Walter George decided to hold out.

Barker waited until the promoter had sold out the entire Coliseum on South Wabash Avenue for a major prize fight. Then, just before the fight was to begin, a half dozen cabs pulled up to the coliseum and let out building inspectors, fire marshals, electrical inspectors, plumbing inspectors and health inspectors, all led by Red Barker. Within minutes after entering the building the inspectors declared that the water was unhealthy to drink and ordered it turned off. The hot dog, beer and soda concessions were shut down by the fire marshal and the electrical inspector said the wiring was faulty and ordered the stadium lights shut off. During the delay, the crowd became violent. George turned to Barker and said "All right, how much you bastard?"

Barker answered that his price was up to $20 per usher and that the minimum number of ushers needed for the night was 120. Barker was paid and the fight went on.

Roger Touhy and Matt Kolb had their own plans for Chicago's labor unions. Prohibition, gambling and the ability to avoid big political payoffs and long drawn out beer wars had made them rich. By 1932, they had the money, and the firepower to take over the entire Chicago Teamsters organization without having to split any of it with Capone.

Unlike Capone, they didn't need to terrorize their way into each local union before reaching the Teamsters International office. They had a direct and trusted contact in the International office with Edward Chicken McFadden, an old time labor terrorist with deep contacts into the Teamsters International leadership.

McFadden picked up the name Chicken when he organized a shakedown operation known as the Kosher Chicken Pluckers Union. He had an arrest record dating back to 1901 that included intent to rob, police impersonation and labor slugging. He had been a business partner with a labor mobster named "Big Tim" Lynch, controlling the Chauffeurs and Teamsters Union together, until Capone had Lynch killed. Capone took over the union and chased McFadden and his contacts into the waiting arms of Roger and Tommy Touhy. In early 1932, when Capone started his major push against the unions, it was McFadden who set up a meeting between the Touhys and Patty Burrell, the Teamsters International Vice President. Burrell called a meeting of all the locals threatened by the syndicate and gave them a choice; they could stand alone against Capone and lose their unions and probably their lives, or they could band together and move their operations into Touhy's camp.

Most of the bosses already knew Roger and decided he was the lesser of the two evils. They pitched into a $75,000 protection fund that was handed over to Tommy Touhy. In exchange, the union bosses were allowed to keep their locals, and the treasuries that came with them, and live under the Touhys' protection.

"Ten Percent Tony"

"Tony Cermak was an example of the lowest type of machine politics that the corrupt political life of Chicago had yet produced. He was uncouth, gruff, insolent and inarticulate . . . he could engage in no more intelligent discussion of the larger political issues of the day than he could of the Einstein theory of relativity. He appeared to take pride in his lack of polish."

—Judge Lyle

Like Matt Kolb, Roger Touhy was a cautious man. He was not prone to mistakes or leaps in judgement, especially when it came to defying a man as dangerous as Al Capone. In fact, the only reason he would have entered a shooting war against Capone and his massive criminal organization was based on his absolute certainty that he would win. That, and his little known agreement with Chicago's powerful mayor, Anton Cermak, made the bootlegger positive that he could pull Capone from his throne.

"Ten Percent" Tony Cermak, the mayor of

Chicago, would lead the Touhys into a war with the Capone syndicate. Tony Cermak was, as Judge Lyle noted, "not a nice man." Instead he was an intimidator and a bully with a violent temper, who would never walk away from a confrontation. He liked very few people and trusted no one. As his power grew, so did his paranoia. In the state house, as president of Cook County and later as mayor, Cermak used wiretaps, stolen mail, secret surveillance and informants to get intelligence on the weaknesses of his enemies.

Cermak was born on May 7, 1873 in a Bohemian village about fifty miles from Prague. The family immigrated to America in 1884, settling in a Chicago slum. In 1900, the Cermak family moved to Braidwood, in southern Illinois, where the elder Cermak worked as a coal miner. At age sixteen Tony returned to Chicago alone and saw his opportunity in the rough and tumble world of ethnic politics. He organized the Bohemian community into a powerful voting machine and before he was old enough to vote himself, Tony Cermak was a political power in the Windy City.

In addition to his unquenchable thirst for power, Cermak was also a greedy man who used his power and position to grow wealthy. While still a ward politician, he formed the United Societies, a high-sounding name for what was nothing more then a shakedown operation to collect money from the hundreds of pimps and saloon owners who worked along the notoriously wicked 22nd Street (which was later, oddly enough, renamed Cermak Road).

In 1902, at age twenty-six, Cermak went to the State Capitol as a member of the House of Representatives. He eventually worked his way up to Speaker of the House. This position allowed him, if he wished, to block every piece of banking reform legislation before the House. It was a position for which the state's bankers paid him richly. After three terms in the capitol, Cermak's net worth was more than one million dollars. By the time he became mayor of Chicago at age fifty-six, Tony Cermak, the nearly illiterate immigrant, boasted a net worth of seven million dollars, although he never had a job that paid him more then $12,000 a year.

In 1931, Cermak was the undisputed boss of the most powerful political machine in the country, and declared himself a candidate for Mayor of Chicago. The syndicate, sensing the federal government might step in to restore order to the streets of Chicago if the hopelessly corrupt "Big Bill" Thompson was re-elected, stood solidly behind Cermak's candidacy. Ten Percent Tony Cermak the syndicate figured, was one of them. They could live and prosper with Cermak at the helm. On election day, April 7, 1931, Cermak trounced Thompson by the largest margin ever recorded in a Chicago mayoral election. He promised the people of Chicago that he would rid their city of gangsters before the Century of Progress Exhibition opened at the World's Fair in the summer of 1933. But Cermak wouldn't rid Chicago of organized crime. Instead he would try to corral it, dominate it, and grow rich from it. All he had to do was give it another face, a plot the federal government had unknowingly aided by putting Capone in prison on a shaky tax charge. Capone's imprisonment left a void in Chicago's crime syndicate. Cermak intended to fill that void with Roger Touhy.

Touhy had told Saul Alinsky, a sociologist, writer and former member of the Joliet State Prison parole board, that in 1932 he entered a partnership with Cermak to run Chicago's underworld. The middle man in the deal was Teddy Newberry, a thug who at one time or another had been associated with every major gang in the city and acted as Cermak's bag man on the street.

In a meeting at the mayor's office, Cermak and Newberry urged Touhy to wage a war with Capone's mob. Roger was reluctant. A defensive position against the mob was one thing, but an all out war was entirely different. The syndicate could, Touhy pointed out, muster at least 500 gunmen in a few days. Cermak responded, "You can have the entire police department."

Eventually, Roger agreed to go along, and Cermak sent word to his police commanders that the Touhys were to be cooperated with in the war against the syndicate.

Wars cost money. Before the shooting started Roger had to be positive that the cash he needed to support a street war was in place. Anton Cermak could help with that.

At 6:56 A.M., on December 6, 1932, Tommy Touhy led a gang of five masked men into the United States Post Office in the heart of Chicago's Loop. They overpowered the guard and stole $500,000 in securities and cash. The getaway was easy. Two hours earlier, Cermak called the police shift commander and ordered him to pull all of his men out of the area. A month later the Touhys, armed with machine guns, robbed a Minneapolis postal truck of $78,417 in bonds, cash, certificates and jewelry. Several days later they struck again, robbing a Colorado mail truck of $520,000 in cash.

During that time Cermak increased his raids on syndicate gambling dens. In one afternoon alone,

Chicago police acting on Cermak's orders impounded 200 syndicate slot machines plus another 300 machines stored at Gottleib and Company warehouses. This was the same Gottleib that would later provide slots to mob-owned Las Vegas casinos. As soon as the police took the syndicate's machines, Touhy's men replaced them with their own one armed bandits. The moment a Mob handbook was closed Touhy's operators were moved in to fill the gap. As always, Cermak had an ulterior motive. The raids were a calculated move to cut the syndicate's cash flow in half so that they wouldn't have the funding to carry on a drawn out street war.

It didn't take the mob's leadership a long time to figure out they had been double-crossed by Cermak, who, along with Touhy, was now putting on the double squeeze. The quick solution for the syndicate was to kill Roger and Tommy Touhy. However killing them wouldn't prove easy, especially now that they were surrounded by a small army of enforcers including George "Baby Face" Nelson, a proven tough guy.

Still, the syndicate's bosses were determined to stop the flow of union treasuries to Touhy. To do that, they would have to send out a message; they had to throw a scare into the union bosses. It had to be loud and violent and it had to be someone close to Touhy.

Bill Rooney was just the right person.

William James Rooney was a labor goon who had done his first prison time back in 1907. In the years that followed Rooney would face dozens of arrests including one in 1910 for the suspected murder of Joseph Patrick Shea. Shea had been the business agent for the Chicago sheet metal workers' union, a local which Rooney was trying to muscle his way into. He was acquitted of the murder, even though he had shot Shea dead in the middle of the union hall in front of at least 150 witnesses. No one testified against him and Rooney was released to continue his takeover of the union. By 1928, he not only controlled the sheet metal workers', but the flat janitors' and the meat cutters' unions as well. Capone sent word that he wanted half of Rooney's labor empire. Rooney refused and Capone threatened his life. Unfazed, Rooney made his own threats and then started to move his operation and his family out to Des Plains to live under Touhy's protection.

On the night they killed him, Rooney was still moving his belongings from his home in Chicago to a rented house in Des Plains. His wife and two children had already driven to the country.

Rooney waited outside his home while his chauffeur sprinted down the street to retrieve his car from a rented garage about five minutes away. Draped in a heavy grey top coat and dress hat, Rooney paced back and forth on the lawn as a blue sedan pulled up to the curb. One of the men in the back seat, believed to be Paul Ricca, rolled down a window and said, "Hi Billy."

When Rooney stepped up to the car and bent down to look inside, a shotgun appeared in the window and three blasts ripped into Rooney's head, chest and stomach. Remarkably, the blast didn't knock him down. Instead, Rooney grabbed the car as it sped away, but then slid slowly to his knees. He was dragged twenty-five feet before releasing his grip.

With Rooney dead, Red Barker and Murray Humpreys took over the sheet metal and the building service employees' union and looted its treasury.

Rooney's murder was one of the last bright

moments for the syndicate. For the next two years, the Touhy-Cermak-Newberry combination pounded the mob mercilessly. In fact, within three days of Rooney's murder, the Touhys responded by killing Johnny Genaro, Capone's new acting chief of staff, and his driver, Joey Vince, by pulling up along the side of Genaro's car and drilling a dozen rounds of machine gun fire into both of them.

Genero died immediately but Vince managed to live until the cops arrived. A patrolman lifted the hood's head out of a pool of blood and whispered "Who shot you? Who did this?"

For a man full of bullet holes on the threshold of death, Vince was remarkably lucid. He sat upright for a second and said "I can't describe the men. I was too confused at the moment it happened...and I would never tell you anyway, you piece of shit."

Then he fell back into the gutter and died.

A few days later, Roger Touhy, armed with a machine gun, walked into a meeting at the Teamsters Headquarters in Chicago. With him was his top enforcer, Willie Sharkey, and two other men. Each of them carried a machine gun and a pistol as they herded the union officials and lined them up against the wall. As more members entered the building for a special emergency meeting, they too were lined up against the wall until there were over one hundred members held hostage.

After two hours, Roger stood before the crowd and spoke.

"Listen up you mugs, we've come here today to clean the dago syndicate out of the Teamsters Union."

A cheer went up across the room from the membership. Roger looked over the faces in the hall and spotted a half dozen of Murray Humpreys' enforcers including Artie Barrett whom Touhy had known from the Valley. "We thought you were a right guy" he said to Barrett. "What are you doing hanging around these rats for?"

"Well, hell, I gotta eat Rog," Barrett said.

He let Barrett leave but pulled two of the syndicate's union leaders named Goldberg and Sass into an office and told them to call Murray Humpreys and tell him to come to the building as soon as he could. When they said they couldn't remember the number, Roger said, "Well, get together and think it up or we'll give it to you right outside the door. None of you other mugs have to be afraid, we're after Klondike O'Donnell, Camel Humpreys and Jack White and we won't hurt anybody else."

Out of ignorance or fear Goldberg and Sass didn't place the call.

Roger rounded up his men and left the building at 11:30 in the morning, three full hours after they had arrived, taking Goldberg and Sass with him. His last words to the membership were, "These two are going to get theirs." Once again the membership exploded in cheers.

Sass and Goldberg were released two days later. They were not harmed or abused. "Actually," said Goldberg, "they treated us well. The food was excellent. The conversation was good."

Touhy's brazen daylight raid on the heart of the syndicate's union operation was a slap in the face for Red Barker and Murray Humpreys. The syndicate, less than several hundred in number, had ruled over Chicago's massive unions by fear and the threat of violence. Touhy's raid had temporarily taken away that edge and they needed to get it back.

Barker and Humpreys retaliated with a daylight drive-by shooting at Wall's Bar-B-Que and Rib.

Wall's was a restaurant frequented by the Touhys because Roger had developed a friendship with a waitress, Peggy Carey. In the middle of a sun-filled Saturday afternoon, four carloads of syndicate gunmen sped by the restaurant while Roger and several of his men lounged around in the parking lot. They sprayed the lot and the restaurant with machine gun fire. The Touhys returned fire but remarkably, no one was injured in the melée.

In retaliation for the shooting the Touhys struck The Dells, a large syndicate speakeasy and casino operating just inside Touhy's territory. It was under the protection of a hood named Fred Pacelli, younger brother of future United States Congressman Bill Pacelli. Three of Roger's best men, Willie Sharkey, Roy Marshalk and George Wilke arrived at The Dells driving Roger Touhy's new Chrysler sedan. They walked into the casino, surrounded Pacelli and fired one round into his face and one into the small of his back. After the hood's girlfriend, Maryanne Bruce, tried to wrestle the pistol out of Marshalk's hand they fired a round into her head as well.

A few days later, the Touhys gunned down Red Barker. It was a damaging blow to the syndicate. Willie Sharkey, Roger's most reliable killer, had rented an apartment overlooking Barker's office and waited there patiently, perched in a window, with a water-cooled, tripod set machine gun. Sharkey killed Barker by firing thirty-six bullets into him in a matter of seconds as he walked down the street.

At almost exactly the same time across town, Touhy's gunners, dressed as Chicago police and riding in a borrowed police cruiser, killed a syndicate enforcer named "Fat Tony" Jerfitar, and his partner, Nicky Provenzano. The drive by shooting occurred as the two hoods sat in front of a store with their eyes closed, sun bathing their faces. They never knew what hit them.

Next, Touhy's gang killed a beer peddler named James J. Kenny. He was found in an alley dead, having had the back of his head blown off. A few weeks before the murder the Touhys had taken the unusual step of warning Kenny not to push the syndicate's booze inside their kingdom. He did it anyway, so they killed him.

Four days later an unknown hood, believed to be a professional killer imported from New York by Frank Nitti, was found dead on a Chicago sidewalk. His face was blown off by shotgun pellets. His frozen body was planted, literally, in a snow bank on a dead end street.

A week later, Joe Provenzo, a syndicate soldier, was killed when two men wearing police uniforms asked him his name. When he answered, they thanked him, shot him through the head and calmly walked away. Five minutes later and several blocks away, John Liberto, another Nitti hood, was shot in the head at close range by the same two men.

After that the syndicate took two more hard hits. At the crack of dawn Cermak was in his office, surrounded by his special squad and the Chicago chief of police, planning the day's raids against the mob's most lucrative casinos. Over the remainder of the morning, working on information provided by Roger Touhy and Teddy Newberry, twelve mob casinos were closed down. Sixteen Chicago detectives were demoted, reassigned or fired for allowing a rising syndicate hood named "Tough Tony" Capezio to operate in their districts. The loss of sixteen cops, all bought and paid for, hurt the syndicate badly, leaving them with very few officers on the take.

Cermak's pressure on the police department had scared most officers off the syndicate's pad, while the others waited on the sidelines to see who would come out on top in this war.

The next blow came when two of the syndicate's best gunners, Nicholas Maggio, and his partner in crime, Anthony Persico, were targeted in a retaliation killing for the murder of Bill Rooney. John Rooney, the business agent for the billposters' union and brother to Bill Rooney, ambushed and killed the two men on a back stretch of road deep inside Touhy's territory.

The syndicate was taking a pounding. Their ranks were already thinned from assaults by the federal government, not to mention the beating they were taking at the hands of the Touhy organization. To bolster their numbers the outfit's leaders recruited members of the 42s, a gang of crazy kids from an Italian neighborhood called the Patch. This same gang would produce the syndicate's next ruling body in the form of Sam Giancana, Marshal Ciafano, Teets Battaglia and others.

Reinforced with the 42s, the syndicate tracked down a top Touhy enforcer named Frank Schaeffler, once a contender for the world's light heavy-weight crown. They shot him as he entered an all-night speakeasy called The Advance.

The Touhy forces struck back by killing a major syndicate pimp named Nicky Renelli and in a separate incident gunning down Elmer Russel, a bouncer at a syndicate bar called the Alaskan Forum Road House.

The next mob hood to die was Maurice Barrett. He was shot through the head and arm, then dropped at the front door of a neighborhood hospital where he bled to death.

Three days later the Touhys lined up three of Nitti's men and shot them through the knees with machine guns after they tried to muscle into a meeting at the Chicago house painters' union.

The Touhys scored another big hit when they killed Danny Cain, the thirty-two-year-old president of the Chicago Coal Teamsters and brother-in-law of George Red Barker. Several men in a car followed Cain home as he left a nightclub. They pulled up alongside his car and drowned it in machine gun fire.

On a freezing Wednesday night, Willie O'Brien, a slugger employed by the Touhys, walked into a popular speakeasy called the Garage. There he was jumped by three men who tried to force him outside to the rear alley where a car was waiting. O'Brien managed to fight them all off until one of the men pulled a pistol and fired a shot into O'Brien's back. Unarmed, O'Brien was running toward the front door when another shot caught him in the leg and a third shot went into the palm of his right hand as he used it to cover his spine. A half an hour later O'Brien staggered into the waiting room of the Augustana hospital.

Officer Martin O'Malley, who grew up with Touhy and O'Brien in the Valley, arrived and interviewed the hood on his death bed.

"Who shot you Billy?"

"I known them. Known them for ten years, but I won't tell you who they are."

"You're going to die Billy. Who killed you? I'll have your revenge."

O'Brien just shook his head and died.

Seven days later, the Touhys struck back. It was fifteen degrees below zero and snowing when a car pulled up to the curb. Several men in long coats climbed out, walked into a pool room and poured five shots into a syndicate hood named Fred Petilli who was leaning against a pool table, his back to the door. A few moments later the same car pulled up in front of The Garage nightclub where Jimmy O'Brien had been killed. A tall man, probably Basil Banghart, opened the front door to the club, tossed in a bomb and said "This is for Jimmy, you bastards!"

The bomb blew the place to bits but remarkably, no one was killed.

After that, Charlie O'Neill, a very young Touhy gunman, was kidnapped off the street, shot twice in the head and dumped in the middle of traffic on a busy intersection.

The Touhys responded by killing a labor goon named Nichols Razes. They shot him five times during a running gun battle in the Green Hut restaurant owned by Razes' brother. Charles McKenna, a Touhy labor enforcer and president of the truck painters' union, was shot in the arm during the gun battle. He was arrested for murder as he straggled down the street, murder weapon still in hand. He was held, booked and then released for "lack of evidence."

That same month, the syndicate tried to kidnap Roger Touhy's two sons as they waited for their mother to pick them up from school in Des Plains. Somebody had to pay for that and Roger chose Eddie Gambino, a dope peddler and union goon. They caught Gambino as he was about to step out of his car. Two gunmen, stepped up to the driver's window and opened fire. Before he bled to death, Gambino was able to pull his own pistol but dropped it before he could fire at his killers. One of the two killers, enraged at Gambino's defiance, stepped back over to the hood's blood-smeared face and fired at his temple.

By the spring of 1933 the impossible was happening: the mouse was eating the lion. The Touhys were beating the syndicate.

Nitti

Tony Cermak and Teddy Newberry, probably acting on Touhy's advice, decided that the quickest way to end the gang war was to kill the Capone outfit's new leader, Frank Nitti. After that they figured all the other hoods would fall into line and the two-year-old war would be ended.

Nitti became boss of the Chicago mob through attrition. In the winter of 1931 the federal government started its crackdown on Capone and his operation. On the freezing morning of February 28, 1931, seventy-five heavily armed United States Marshals rounded up and deported more than 125 Capone hoods who had entered the country illegally. There were no long and costly trials, appeals or delays. The gangsters were handcuffed, shoved into an airplane, flown to New York and then shipped back to Europe.

The federal government's lethal use of deportation as a weapon against organized crime had begun. A few days later, on March 13, 1931 a grand jury indicted Capone for tax evasion. Over the next twenty-four months the Treasury Department would effectively close down Capone's syndicate by locking away the organization's top leadership. On November 7, 1931, Al's brother Ralph Capone would go to prison because of a tax conviction. Jake Guzak, Mops Volpe, Murray Humpreys and even Capone's financier, Louis Lipschultz, were eventually indicted and convicted on tax charges along with their boss.

The next in line was Frank Nitti.

Francisco Raffele Nitto, or Frank Nitti as he preferred, was a frail, pensive little man with ulcers and a nervous twitch. He was born outside Palermo, but avoided discussing his Sicilian background, preferring to have himself called "Italian."

Unlike Capone, Nitti was fairly well educated, having trained as a chemist before arriving in Chicago by way of New York. He worked as a barber for a while in the immense Italian community but quickly turned to fencing stolen gems brought to him by his life long friend Louis Greenberg. It was Greenberg who had introduced Nitti to Capone.

The newspaper called Nitti "The Enforcer," but for those who knew the real story, the name was comical. As far as anyone knows, Nitti never killed anyone. Instead, he made his way up through the mob's ranks because he was smart, pushy and cunning. While it was true that he would easily order a beating or an execution by the goon squads he controlled, syndicate leaders rightly considered Nitti a nervous, high-strung individual, better suited, as Paul Ricca once said, "to be the barber-fence he had been."

At mid-morning on the day Cermak decided to have Frank Nitti killed, His Honor summoned two members of his special squad to his office, Harry Miller and Henry Lang. Miller, who had once been dismissed from the police force for trafficking narcotics, was the youngest of the notorious Miller brothers who headed the Valley Gang. Lang had been a bag man for former Mayor Big Bill Thompson and taught Miller the little bit he needed to know about being a crook when he came on the force by "special political appointment" back in 1927. Now, both men were detective sergeants on Cermak's "Special Squad," a group of tough cops with questionable backgrounds, brought together to carry out Cermak's every whim.

At 10:00 in the morning on December 20, 1932, Cermak called Miller and Lang to his office. When they arrived, Teddy Newberry was already there sitting on the mayor's desk smoking one of his small cigars. Newberry handed them a slip of paper with Frank Nitti's name and office address on it and told them that it was time for Nitti to die. Miller and Lang were commissioned for the task. He said that once Nitti was dead he would pay them $15,000 each. That was good money for a pair of cops who were supposed to be making less than one hundred dollars a week.

Lang and Miller drove to Nitti's office at the La Salle-Wacker building and flagged down a passing squad car. "We might need some help inside," they told the driver, a rookie cop named Chris Callahan. Then the three men entered the massive office building and took the elevator to the fifth floor, room 554, where Nitti kept a cramped, three-room office. When they entered the room they found Nitti, his bodyguard and several others gathered around a desk. Lang ordered them to turn and face the wall with their hands raised over their heads. Lang then grabbed Nitti by the wrists and ordered Callahan to search him.

"When I bent down to grab Nitti's ankles," Callahan said, "Lang fired five shots into Nitti. I leaped back. Nitti staggered toward the door and then he stopped and looked at Lang, and he said 'What's this for?' and Lang shot him again. Then Lang walked to an anteroom, alone, and fired a single shot. When he came back out, he was shot through the hand."

Nitti had been shot in the neck, leg and groin. He was taken to Bridewell Hospital, where his father-in-law, Dr. Gaetano Ronga, was called to care for him. After several hours Dr. Ronga emerged from the operating room to announce that Frank Nitti would probably die before the night was over.

Nitti lived and, while it was true that the shooting had panicked what was left of Capone's leadership, it was now only a matter of days before they reorganized and struck back. The good news for Touhy was that Murray Humpreys, Red Barker's assistant, did not fight being jailed on federal income tax charges, no doubt to avoid sure death at the hands of the Touhys. The bad news was that the shooting put a far more competent and dangerous man in charge of the outfit in the form of Paul "the Waiter" Ricca. Ricca's first move was to bring in "Three Fingers" Jack White to replace the murdered Red Barker.

White was a Valley Gang graduate who said he got his nickname when a brick fell on his hand on a construction site when he was a boy, crushing several fingers. It was a deformity he tried to hide with a glove, stuffing the empty fingers with cotton. In fact it's more likely that White lost the fingers in a bungled burglary attempt where he mishandled nitroglycerin, a common mishap that probably cost Roger Touhy his right thumb as well. White recruited James "Fur" Sammons, a certified psychopath and probably the most dangerous man in Chicago, if not in the United States.

Like White, Sammons' record was long and varied. In 1900 he and four others kidnaped an eleven-year-old, eighty-five-pound school girl, raped her, broke her nose, punched out one of her eyes and stabbed her in the vaginal area with a pencil. Sammons, who showed no remorse over the attack, smirked at the girl's parents in court. He was given five years for his part in the crime and was paroled two years later. Two months after his release, Sammons was arrested for the murder of Patrick Barret, a saloon keeper. He was convicted and sentenced to be hanged. He was put into solitary confinement where it was said he was driven insane by the solitude. He remained on death row until 1917 when he managed to escape and commit a series of robberies before being recaptured.

Both Three Fingers Jack White and Sammons had been paroled in 1923 by Illinois Governor Len Small after paying a small fortune in bribe money to "Porky" Dillon, a Touhy gunman who had been one of Small's bagmen. Porky Dillon had an interesting background. He had once been sentenced to serve ten years in the state prison but managed to rig a pardon for himself from the same corrupt governor, Small.

White was a competent battle tactician. Now backed by Sammons' psychotic brutality, he was able to take back the upper hand in the battle against the Touhys in four quick and deadly blows. The first to die under the White-Sammons regime was Teddy Newberry, the mayor's bag man who plotted the Nitti shooting. Newberry was found lying face down in a ditch of frozen water in Porter

County, Indiana. The killers were on their way to a mob burial ground, the gruesome real estate that belonged to "Machine Gun" Jack McGurn and was later passed down to Mickey "the Ant" Spilotro in the 1970s.

Next they got Touhy's strongest ally, Paddy Barrell. Barrell was the international vice president of the Teamsters. He was killed while he and his bodyguard, Willie Marks, were vacationing in Wisconsin. Marks, a former Moran gunner, had survived the St. Valentine's Day Massacre by being late for work. This time he wasn't so lucky. The killer, believed to be Fur Sammons, caught Barrell and Marks off guard while the two were fishing knee deep in a lake. The blast from the shotgun, fired only inches from the victims, nearly took off Barrell's head.

A second and awesome setback for the Touhys came when White and Sammons caught Matt Kolb at his saloon, the Club Morton. Kolb was standing in the hallway next to a roulette wheel. Walking up from behind him, Sammons said, "Hello Matt." As Kolb reached out to shake hands, Sammons grabbed his hand and arm tightly as White pulled out an automatic and poured the six shots into the little fat man. After the killers started to leave, Sammons said, "I better make sure." He returned and fired another shot into Kolb's head. The final round picked up the dead man's skull and bounced it off the floor. With Kolb dead and his blackmail records gone, the price for political and police protection went through the roof, even with Cermak on their side.

The next blow came when Tommy Touhy was gunned down by Fur Sammons. It happened when Tommy and two cars of his men combed the streets of Chicago looking for Fur Sammons. As it turns out

Sammons was out in an armor-plated car, looking for Tommy. The two groups spent several hours stalking each other until Tommy decided that he had had enough of the cat and mouse game and ordered his caravan to pull over at the intersection and wait for Sammons.

Several minutes later Sammons brazenly pulled up alongside them, Tommy leaned out his window, machine gun in hand and opened fire on Sammons, hitting his tires and radiator. Then, without taking his finger off the trigger, Tommy climbed out of his car and stood on the bumper and fired into Sammons' windows. Sammons leaned out of his window and released a clip into Tommy's legs while driving with one hand and firing with the other. A squad car from the town of River Forrest pulled onto the scene and demanded that the gunmen pull over. The Touhys answered by firing a clip off at the cops who returned fire, but by then Touhy and Sammons had disappeared into the city.

Tommy Touhy was cut up badly. This was a major setback for the Cermak-Touhy operation since Tommy was the organization's field general. Unlike the pensive and remote Roger, Tommy was earthy and gregarious, gifted with a natural charisma that his group trusted. He was their motivator. Without him, the gang was in trouble.

Despite the recent small victories that White had scored for the syndicate it was undeniable that the mouse was still eating the lion. Against all odds, the Touhy-Cermak combination was winning the street war. The 42 Gang, the syndicate's front-line troops, were tough and fearless, but they were wild and undisciplined and the Touhys were picking them off with ease. Other, more seasoned syndicate hoods were turning up dead at the rate of one every other day. The *Chicago Tribune* put the number of casualties as high as seventy dead in one six-month period. At the same time, the federal government was closing in on the syndicate, deporting hundreds of reliable operatives and throwing most of the remaining syndicate power players in jail.

Although the Touhys had taken their share of a beating, they could hold out in the fight for a couple years more. They were smaller, tighter and more organized than the remains of Capone's mob and they had the resources to hire the best gunmen money could buy.

Chasing the syndicate out of the Teamsters had assured them ready access to the union's enormous pension fund, and the Teamsters' top leadership was backing Touhy's war against the syndicate.

Then there was Tony Cermak, who remained Touhy's strongest ally. As long as they had Cermak on their side, they controlled the police and City Hall.

It was clear to Paul Ricca that the key to ending the war was to kill Anton Cermak. For its inability to take back the streets from Touhy, Chicago looked ridiculous in the eyes of the new national crime syndicate. Worse yet, the New York mobs were taking advantage of the disorder in Chicago by planting their flags in Los Angeles, Florida, Arkansas, Nevada and Texas. They had to kill Cermak. The war had to end.

The Guns of Zangara

"Touhy had the syndicate on the ropes and they were ready to throw in the sponge but then they killed Anton Cermak."

—Saul Alinsky

Anton Cermak had an animal's instinct for survival, and after the failed attempt on Frank Nitti's life, he knew his own days were numbered. In fact, a few weeks after the botched murder attempt, Louis "Short Pants" Campagna, Capone's former bodyguard who had risen to syndicate chief, had personally planned Cermak's murder, almost succeeding in gunning him down in an early morning ambush inside the Loop.

Cermak tried to postpone the inevitable by beefing up his bodyguard detail from two to five men and augmenting them with private security forces. He also took the added precaution of moving from the accessible Congress Hotel to the more secluded Morrison, where he paid for a private elevator that went nonstop to his penthouse suite.

It didn't matter how careful he was. They were going to kill him. They had to kill him. They planned to kill Touhy, too but that could wait because they knew that wouldn't end the war. Cermak would just replace him with another ambitious hood. Murdering Cermak was the key. Kill the head and the body dies.

While it was true that there was a huge risk in killing the mayor of the second largest city in the United States, it was the key to their survival and maybe, just maybe, they would get away with it. A Chicago mayor had been gunned down in the past. Chicago's mayor Henry Harrison was killed in October, 1893. The shooter was one Eugene Pendergast, who claimed that the mayor had reneged on a political appointment.

The syndicate knew the shooter they found would have to be a "nutcase" as they put it, but they could find a patsy to take the fall. That was the easy part. It was all a matter of timing and opportunity, both of which came together when Anton Cermak announced that he would greet President-elect Roosevelt in a public park in Florida.

Finding the patsy to take the blame for the murder fell to Paul the Waiter Ricca. Ricca earned his nickname while working in a restaurant owned by his mentor "Diamond Joe" Esposito, a colorful underworld character whose deep political contacts enabled him to finagle a federal license to import sugar from Cuba into the states. Sugar, and lots of it, was the primary ingredient needed to make bootleg whisky.

Esposito was a major player in the underworld. With the money he made by importing sugar, Esposito was able to expand his criminal holdings into the control of several vital teamster unions which he flatly refused to share with Capone. So they killed him. He was shot on the street while his wife and two small children watched.

As a reward for setting up his boss for the kill, Capone allowed Ricca to take over most of Esposito's operations including the legal and profitable sugar importing business which Ricca handed over to a young hood named Dave Yaras from Chicago's west side. Ricca invested in Yaras' move to Florida and in exchange got a handsome cut of all of Yaras' illegal ventures, including a piece of his narcotics smuggling ring based out of Havana. Within a year after his arrival, Yaras' rackets in south Florida and Cuba were second only to Meyer Lansky's in size and profitability.

According to mob boss Sam Giancana, it was Yaras who decided that Cermak's killer would be Giuseppe Zangara, a thirty-two-year-old bricklayer who preferred to be known by his Americanized name of Joey Zangara.

Giuseppe Zangara was a mean, near-illiterate, sullen little hood from Southern Italy. He arrived in America in 1923 and took up residence with an uncle in Paterson, New Jersey.

In September of 1929, Zangara and a syndicate hood, Tony Adgostino, were arrested for violating the prohibition law by running a 1,000-gallon still in Mount Vail, New Jersey. At the station house, Zangara claimed his name was Luigi DiBernardo and pleaded guilty, telling the police he owned the still, thus allowing the higher-ranking Adgostino to walk away from prosecution. For his troubles, Zangara was sentenced to one year and a day at Atlanta Federal Prison. During sentencing, United States Attorney Philip Forman, later a federal judge, asked "Your real name is Zangara, isn't it?"

leaving the implication that Zangara was no stranger to the courtroom. Off the record, the bootlegger admitted that he was Giuseppe Zangara but that he would enter prison under the assumed name of Luigi DiBernardo. Several years later, when the United States Secret Service investigated the Cermak shooting, agents compared photographs of DiBernardo the bootlegger with Zangara the assassin and determined that they matched. Remarkably, the agent never followed up the lead.

Paroled from prison in 1931, Zangara moved to south Florida where he kept to himself. One of his few known contacts was his roommate, an Italian immigrant named Joseph Patane who worked at Valentino's restaurant in Miami, a mob hangout. Patane was introduced to Zangara by their landlady, Constantina Vatrone, a Sicilian immigrant whose husband Petro Vatrone had been active in the mob in Florida until he was stabbed to death in 1924, in what she later told the Secret Service was "an underworld incident."

Zangara spent most of his time gambling and losing heavily. In need of cash, he took a position as a mule, or courier, in Dave Yaras' heroin smuggling operation, working out of a narcotics processing plant in south Florida. Zangara's job was to transport the drugs up to New York where he turned them over to distribution specialists like Ben "Bugsy" Siegel in Brooklyn, Abner "Longy" Zwillman in New Jersey and others who would pay for the delivery. In turn, Zangara was supposed to hand the cash over to Yaras.

But, according to several published reports, while Zangara was on one of his runs he made off with the mob's money and lost it at the track. Yaras decided to kill him. Then news came from Chicago

City Hall that his Honor, Anton J. Cermak, would make an appearance in Miami's Bayfront Park to greet President-elect Roosevelt.

Anton Cermak would make a public appearance in a crowded, open area. It was a godsend for the mob. Ricca sent word down to Yaras that they were going to kill Cermak at the park and that Yaras was to line somebody up to take the fall for the murder. It was too big a hit to not leave a gunman to take the blame. The shotgun killing of Cook County's Assistant States Attorney Billy McSwiggin a few years before had taught them a valuable lesson: always leave a fall guy.

Yaras called Zangara into his office, and gave him his two dismal choices. The mob could kill him, or Zangara could take his chances and shoot Cermak for them. Maybe the cops would kill him, or maybe the crowd would rip him to pieces, or maybe he'd get lucky. Maybe he'd get caught after he killed Cermak. He could claim he was insane and if the judge and jury bought it, at the most he might get ten maybe fifteen years in an insane asylum and then he could walk, all debts forgiven. Yaras knew what he was talking about. Florida, second only to Texas, had the most lenient laws on the books in dealing with mentally ill criminals.

Zangara chose to kill Cermak and take his chances with an insanity plea or the possibility that he could slip into the crowd and disappear.

As implausible as it might seem, Zangara may have actually believed that he was going to get away with it. After the shooting, when Secret Service agents searched Zangara's room, they found his neatly packed travel bag sitting in the middle of his bed. Inside were his clothes, a book, *The Wehman Brothers' Easy Method for Learning Spanish*

Quickly, several newspaper clippings about Roosevelt's trip to Florida and another on the Lincoln assassination conspiracy.

Despite Zangara's fantasies of escape, the mob had no intentions of letting him slip away and disappear. They needed a patsy to take the fall. They had already started painting a picture of Zangara, the conservative registered Republican, as Zangara, a radical communist who wanted to overthrow the American government. But better than a patsy, they wanted a dead patsy. According to Roger Touhy, the second after Zangara shot Cermak, a mob assassin would shoot Zangara and disappear into the crowd, leaving the Miami police, Secret Service or Cermak's private guards with the credit for killing the Mayor's murderer. The gunman was also there to make sure that Zangara followed through on his assignment. As Chicago newsman Jack Lait wrote, "had Cermak escaped Zangara's bullets, another triggerman would have gotten him."

The two back-up gunmen were Three Fingers Jack White and Al Capone's former bodyguard Frankie Rio, both of whom were picked up at the Chicago train station two days before Anton Cermak was shot. But the police had no reason to hold the two smirking hoods who explained that they were on their way to Florida for a short vacation. "You mugs slay me," White said. "First you ride me to get out of town and then when I try to leave, you want me to stay."

The next day, down in Florida, Giuseppe Zangara went to the Davis pawn shop in downtown Miami and spent eight dollars on a .32 calibre revolver and ten bullets. While still in the shop, Zangara placed five bullets in the chamber and kept five in his pocket and then began stalking Anton Cermak. Zangara walked to the Bostick Hotel because he had read in the papers that the hotel's owners, Horace and May Bostick, were close friends of Cermak and expected him to drop by that evening before he went to Bayfront Park. Zangara went to the hotel, which was actually more of a rooming house than anything else. He paid his dollar for the night and asked to see all of the exits and entrances. Then he went to his room where he proceeded to sit on the edge of the bed, with the door open, and stare down the hallway toward the front door of the hotel, waiting for Anton Cermak to arrive so he could kill him.

At 5:30, after six hours of waiting, Zangara probably realized that Cermak wasn't coming and left the hotel by a back door. He quickly walked several blocks to a cigar manufacturing plant owned by Andrea Valenti, a Sicilian immigrant. Zangara, Valenti and two other men, Steve Valenti and Lorenzo Grandi, left the factory at about 7:30 and made their way to Bayfront Park. But they miscalculated how many people would turn out for the event. By the time they arrived at the park, at about eight o'clock, 10,000 spectators filled it to standing room only. Slowly, and sweating profusely, Zangara and the others obnoxiously pushed and shoved through the crowd trying desperately to make their way to the bandstand.

At about that same time, Anton Cermak was preparing to leave his hotel room for the park. He was dismally sick with peritonitis causing him to double over in pain. A lesser man would have canceled the night's engagement but Tony Cermak had always been extraordinary. As he prepared to put on his light blue and white jacket, a bodyguard handed him a bulky black bullet-proof vest but Cermak didn't want it. It was too humid and he was weak. It was a mistake that would cost him his life.

Cermak arrived at the park about a half-hour before Franklin Roosevelt's car pulled up to the bandstand. At about the same time, Zangara pushed and shoved his way up to the second row of chairs.

F.D.R. placed himself on the car's rear seat. He took a small black microphone and made a short speech as a flood light beamed down on him in his white suit. He was the perfect target, but Zangara, less than thirty-five feet away, never fired.

When Roosevelt's speech ended, he turned and looked up at the stage and saw Cermak sitting in the front row and waved "Tony! Come on down here."

Smiling broadly, Cermak rose from his chair and walked toward F.D.R., his bodyguards stepping up to join him, but Cermak told them to stay where they were. It was unseemly, he said, for the Mayor of Chicago to be photographed with more body-guards than the President-elect.

The two men shook hands and chatted for less than three minutes, then Cermak stepped away from the car and turned to his right and then, for some unknown reason, walked a dozen steps away from the stage and toward the place where Zangara was waiting.

At that moment, Zangara leaped out of the crowd and sprang onto an open seat, drew his revolver from his trouser pocket, fired five rounds directly at Cermak. One bullet hit Cermak in the right armpit and pushed its way to just above his heart and then drove itself into his right lung, causing the mayor to grab his chest with both arms and slowly sink to his knees.

Several other bystanders were struck by bullets, yet Zangara maintained, repeatedly, that he never got off more than three rounds from his five-round pistol. Remarkably, police recovered seven bullets from the scene.

Just minutes after the shooting, United States Representative-elect Mark Wilcox and Chicagoan Robert Gore, told a radio newsman they were standing a few feet from Zangara. Gore said, "He was shooting at Cermak. There is no doubt about that. The killer waited until Mr. Roosevelt sat and then fired."

Based on Gore and Wilcox's statement, reports that Cermak had been shot by Chicago gangsters went out over the wires at once. But after the first day, there was no other mention of gangsters being involved in the shooting. Later, when Roosevelt waited in the halls of the Jackson Memorial Hospital where Cermak was being treated, he pointed out that not one of the six persons hit by bullets were near him when they were shot. In fact they were at least thirty feet away and only two or three feet away from Cermak and, added Roosevelt, Zangara had not fired off a single shot at him while he had a full eight minute window during his speech. Roosevelt concluded that Zangara was "a Chicago gangster" sent to kill Cermak.

In 1959, at his last parole hearing, Roger Touhy said that when Zangara started shooting, Jack White and Frankie Rio, both wearing Cook County Deputy Sheriff's badges, waited until Cermak fell to his knees and then stepped out from the crowd and fired a .45 caliber pistol at Zangara but the shot missed and nicked several bystanders instead. Before they could get off a second shot, the crowd had leaped onto Zangara, in effect saving his life.

From his hospital bed Anton Cermak insisted that he was Zangara's target. When his secretary arrived from Chicago, Cermak said to him, "So you're alive! I figured maybe they'd shot up the office too."

Cermak was in relatively good condition on the first few nights in the hospital and issued his own news bulletins on his condition. By the third day, however, colitis complicated Cermak's wounds and caused him great pain. At one point Cermak's intestinal trouble made his temperature rise to 101.6. On February 27, Cermak contracted pneumonia and died. Giuseppe Zangara went on trial for murder.

Zangara's three lawyers appointed by the state didn't speak Italian, had never tried a criminal case and none of them had ever argued before a jury. It was their recommendation that Zangara plead guilty. When he did, the court sentenced him to death less than two months after he fired the fatal shots that killed Anton Cermak.

His last few days were dismal. The only people to visit him in jail were the prison chaplains, whom he cursed and threw out regularly. Just before he was walked out to the death chamber, the prison warden asked Zangara if he was part of an organized group that plotted to kill Cermak "No. I have no friends. It was my own idea."

Then the little murderer strutted down the hall and sat himself in the electric chair, but he was so short his feet didn't touch the ground. Just before the guards placed a hood over his head Zangara turned to the warden, smirked and yelled "*Viva Italia! Viva comorra!*"

The word *comorra* was one of many Italian terms for the Mafia. Then he leaned back and waited. The room was filled with an uncomfortable silence as 2,300 volts snuffed out Zangara's strange life.

Ed Kelly, Chicago's next mayor, was the kind of city official that Frank Nitti could live with. When reporters were looking to tell Kelly that he was Chicago's new mayor, they found him gambling at a mob owned race track in Havana. When asked if he thought that the syndicate had anything to do with Cermak's killing, Kelly replied "Boys, from now on, there is no such thing as organized crime in the city of Chicago."

9 Prelude to a Hoax

When Roger Touhy learned that the mob had murdered Anton Cermak, he rented a plane and flew to Indianapolis to meet with the leaders of the Teamsters International Council. Roger wanted to plan their next steps in the war against the syndicate. But the meeting didn't go well. The International was pulling out of the fight. It was, in effect, surrendering to the syndicate. The union's leadership felt that although Touhy had won battles, without Cermak's clout behind him he would never win the war.

Without the Teamsters' financial support, Roger knew that the war was lost. The best thing to do was to hold off the syndicate for as long as he could, make as much money as he could, fold up his operation and leave Chicago forever, perhaps living out his dream to retire to the wilds of Colorado.

He had other reasons to worry, too. United States Postal Inspectors were hot on his trail for the string of mail robberies that he and his gang had pulled off the year before. Although the robberies had gone well, the rumor in the underworld was that Gus Winkler, one of the crooks who helped Touhy cash in the stolen mail loot, was informing on him.

Roger decided to plug the leak on October 9, 1934.

"Smiling" Gus Winkler's motto was "Take care of Winkler first." He had spent most of his criminal career doing just that. This was why the Touhys and everyone else connected with the mail robberies wrongly suspected him of being the government's informant in the mail robberies.

Touhy's own spies had reported that Winkler was seen in the FBI's office in the Bankers Building and on the day before they put seventy-two bullets into him he was seen talking with special agent Melvin Purvis on a side street just inside the Loop.

Before Winkler was tied to the case it was widely assumed that Touhy was at odds with him.

Gus Winkler had started out as a member of Eagan's Rats and by age twenty was a safe blower by trade. He did time from 1920-1926, sentenced for assault and wounding with a deadly weapon. He left St. Louis, moved to Chicago and struck up a lifelong friendship with Fred "Killer" Burke, which was how he first came to the attention of Chicago detectives in 1929.

In 1932 Winkler turned over bonds from a Lincoln, Nebraska robbery in which he had played a part to the Secret Six, a group of Chicago business executives who had banded together to take action against the Chicago underworld. When the cops started to close in, Winkler cut a deal and informed on the others so long as he could walk, reasoning that he had always made it clear that he would squeal in order to save himself.

Winkler took Newberry's place in the northside

gangs as a chief financial backer and even moved into Newberry's old apartment at 3300 Lake Shore Drive. In an effort to appear more refined in the later days of his life, he started to wear glasses to cover up his crooked glass eye. He even married a tall, beautiful blonde.

The cops Winkler consorted with were amused by him. It was easy to be amused by Gus Winkler; he was good-natured, smart and a smooth talker. On one of his frequent stops by the detective bureau Winkler told them that he often envisioned his own death by bullets. Most of the cops and criminals in Chicago agreed that Winkler was probably one of the shooters in the St. Valentine's Day massacre, after which he went into seclusion in Cicero where he was said to be in semi-retirement, plotting crimes.

He was widely considered to be too cowardly to execute the crimes he planned. "No man in Chicago history ever played both ends against the middle so adroitly," it was said of him. When Newberry was killed he moved into the Northside gang's leadership and offered shelter and equipment to gangsters on the run.

Winkler was an egomaniac who talked incessantly. Once during a poker game he bragged to his lawyer, Joe Marovitz and the nightclub star, Joe E. Lewis, "You know, I'm the toughest guy in Chicago...maybe the toughest guy in the whole country." Without looking up from his cards Marovitz threw a right cross on to Winkler's chin and knocked him out of his chair.

"Why'd you do that?" Winkler asked.

"To show you that you're not the toughest guy in this room."

Winkler and his wife, "Mother" (as he called her)

had one of the strangest relationships in gangdom. She reviewed each and every illegal endeavor her husband became involved with, first chastising him about the heavenly and earthly illegalities of his work and then for possible slip ups in the plan "Sure, Mother," Winkler would say "You're right, it is an un-Christian act. Now that you've got that load off your chest tell us if the plan is alright."

Gifted with an eagle's eye for detail, she would review a plan over and over again, looking for potential problems before giving her approval. "She's the best I've ever seen," Winkler boasted.

According to Joe E. Lewis, Winkler had one eye shot out during a mail robbery and was convinced that the Touhys were out to kill him because he had "not apportioned the loot equitably." The day before he was killed, Winkler went to the Mayo Clinic in Minnesota with his lawyer, Joe Marovitz and Joe E. Lewis, to let the doctors have a look at Lewis' recently slashed throat. When they returned to Chicago Winkler refused to leave his lawyer's side. "I can't go back to my hotel and I'm afraid to register at a new one. Got any idea where I can go?" he asked Lewis, who gave him the extra key to his suite at the Seneca Hotel.

The next day he was gunned down. Winkler's killer had waited an hour and a half for him outside the beer plant owned by Cook County Commissioner Charles Weber at 1414 Roscoe Street. As Winkler strolled toward Weber's office the killers leaped out of a green truck and fired low; in all seventy-two pellets and bullets went into him in a matter of seconds. He was literally riddled with pellets from his neck to his ankles with most of them going into his back, yet not one bullet hit his head or face. "Turn me over, I can't breathe," he gasped.

He asked for a priest before he died and doctors found a half dozen religious relics pinned to his underwear. He was a big donor to Father Coughlin who sent him the medals. Winkler died begging for God's mercy on his soul, saying the Lord's Prayer to Father James Fitzgerald.

When told that Winkler was dead, a postal inspector threw up his arms and said "Well, this balls up an already balled up case."

The Touhys were suspected of ordering the killing. Hood-for-hire Dominic Marzano was held for questioning and Matt Kolb's old boss, Martin Guifolye, who was now mostly a gambler, was also being sought for questioning. Guifolye called the police and said he was available for questioning at any time. The cops also hauled in Babe Baron, a "0" of Jacob Arvey who was a close friend of international con man John Factor. Baron, a future kingpin for the mob in Las Vegas, was known to have killed Jimmy Walsh in front of Henrici's Restaurant on December 3, 1929. When cops picked him up for questioning in Winkler's death Baron was carrying a pistol in his coat pocket. He was released after several hours. Baron would go on to run one of the city's more successful car dealerships in the 1950s, due in part to a lucrative contract he had to repair city police cars.

Another suspect was Joe Bergi, Winkler's partner in a garage where he fitted cars with bulletproof siding and windows, police lights and sirens that cop cars used in 1933. Baron later took over all the garage businesses.

In September of that year, Bergi was arrested for harboring "Machine Gun" Kelly. Winkler was suspected of having told the police that Bergi was hiding Kelly and provided information about Kelly's role in the Urshel kidnapping case.

As Winkler was a snitch, there were too many suspects for his murder. To this day the crime remains unsolved.

Even with Winkler dead, postal inspectors were able to use the information he provided and move in on the mail robbers. A secret indictment was filed naming Roger Touhy, Gus Schafer and others in his gang as the persons behind the robberies.

Secret or not, Roger got word of the pending indictment. On his lawyer's advice, he decided it was best to leave town until they could work out a way to avoid indictment, either in the courtroom or through bribes.

On July 17, 1933, Roger and four of his men left for a brief working vacation to the north woods of Wisconsin to Rohrbacher's Resort in the lake region. Although avoiding a subpoena was the primary purpose of the trip, the other purpose was to find George Maitland. Maitland was the sole witness in the killing of a syndicate enforcer named John Renelli, whom the Touhys had gunned down several months before. Roger's informants had discovered that Maitland was hiding out in the Lake region, at Renelli's brother's place, The Chicago Tavern. However, when Maitland discovered that Touhy was in the area he quickly fled back to the relative safety of Chicago.

Traveling with Touhy, probably in the capacity of a bodyguard, was thirty-six year old Gustave Schactel, aka Gus Schafer. Jim Ryan, Touhy's top enforcer, had hired Schafer as a guard for his beer collectors in May of 1933 and before long Schafer was planning additional mail robberies for the gang. Schafer's brother, Joseph Schactel, was a Catholic priest and a Ph.D. candidate at the Catholic

University of America in Washington D.C. For years, Gus had managed to keep his criminal life away from his brother.

And what a criminal life it was. Schafer was arrested in San Francisco on December 15, 1913 for burglary, and was sentenced to five years' probation. He was arrested again that same year and sent to prison for attempted larceny and released in 1916. He was arrested again on March 9, 1922, in Oakland for highway robbery and sent to Stillwater Prison in Minnesota on June 16, 1922. After his release he was arrested again on March 16, 1931, in Los Angeles on suspicion of robbery, grand theft auto and was sent to prison in Pontiac, Michigan.

Schafer did more time in the Stillwater, Minnesota prison for a jewelry store robbery. After that, Schafer had been working in San Francisco on gambling boats as "atmosphere" as he put it, from March of 1931 until March 1932 when he and his wife packed their Chevy and relocated to Chicago.

The marriage had problems since its inception in Oakland, California in 1920. When Gus went to prison in Minnesota his wife filed for divorce, but when he was released she dropped the proceedings. Schafer said he went to Chicago to make money on the World's Fair liquor business and felt that "if I didn't make some money my marriage would be on the rocks."

They settled in Oak Park and then Des Plains where they were put up by a German family who had known Schafer's parents in Europe. The family gave them a small apartment. Then in May of 1933 he was brought into the Touhy organization as a hired gun. Roger and Tommy Touhy liked Schafer's style. When they learned that he had been the prison movie projectionist they promoted him to a minor official status in Tommy Maloy's movie projectionists' union so he could explain his income.

The red-headed Schafer was a serious man by nature, seldom smiling. As Touhy said "a big guffaw or belly laugh for him was a slight twitch at the corners of the lips." But Schafer did have a dry, hangman's wit that Tommy and Roger enjoyed.

After Schafer moved to Illinois he brought in Patrick McDonald, a San Francisco gambler whom he had done time with. The two of them, with Touhy's permission, opened a handbook in the Montrose Apartments in Chicago.

The second bodyguard traveling with them was Willie Sharkey, a career criminal and enforcer who had known the Touhys from their days in the Valley. Sharky worked directly for "Chicken" McFadden. Nearly fifty-nine years old, Sharkey was short and pot-bellied like Roger, standing in at only five-feet, four-inches; he sported a four-inch horizontal scar on his left cheek and a two-inch scar on the corner of his right eyelid. Balding, he wore glasses and had a tattoo of a girl's head on his right elbow which winked when he moved his arm in a certain way.

The Touhys liked Sharkey's easygoing manner and good nature when he was sober, but otherwise they considered him dangerous, slightly insane and not very bright.

"Willie had two talents," Touhy said, "getting into jail and buying clothes that didn't fit him. He drank too much and he wasn't too smart, but he had a good heart and I liked him."

Sharkey's third talent was murder. At the time of the trip into the northwoods, Sharkey was wanted for questioning in Chicago in relation to at least five gangland slayings. In 1929 Willie and his brother John Sharkey, who played a role in several of the

Touhys' mail robberies, had opened a saloon just inside the Chicago line with an unknown partner. In 1931, the Capones kicked in the front door to the saloon and gunned down Sharkey's partner. "And since that time," John Sharkey told FBI agent Melvin Purvis, "I moved out of Chicago because of my relationship to my brother, and persons in the syndicate might endeavor to cause me trouble, such as killing me."

Willie Sharkey was a shy man who never married. However, he was proud of his brother and his family and supplemented their income with his own. Willie lived with them in Park Ridge for a while, giving his brother a Lincoln and a Ford.

The fourth person on the trip was Edward Thomas Chicken McFadden, a labor racketeer from the old days. McFadden worked as a food and poultry inspector for the Hoover administration during the first World War. For seventeen years he had been employed as a poultry inspector and contract loader on Water Street in Chicago.

According to Willie Sharkey, McFadden was a friend and business associate of Big Tim Lynch before Lynch was killed. In fact, the 1930 Lincoln Sedan that McFadden drove and registered in his own name was actually owned by Lynch. They were both members of the same union, the Chauffeurs and Teamsters Union of Maywood, Illinois. Sharkey said McFadden stayed on in the union as the business manager but was forced to withdraw in the last part of 1931 after the syndicate made several attempts to kill him.

In his labor organizing days, McFadden was called "Father Tom" since he was prone to try and reason with his quarry in soft, soothing tones before resorting to violence with them.

McFadden had been a friend of Roger's father back when he walked a beat in the Lawndale district. His record dated back to 1901 when he was locked up for intent to rob. Other arrests included police impersonation and labor slugging. In 1931, McFadden was sixty-seven years of age and in ill health. His hearing was gone and he had just recently been released from the Cook County Hospital for a gall bladder problem. Still, McFadden had deep contacts in the labor union field and was the person most responsible for bringing the Teamster unions over to Touhy's side in 1931.

The fifth and sixth persons on the trip were more than probably August J. LaMarr (also known as Jimmy Lamar) and Leroy Marshalk, one of Roger Touhy's best gunmen.

The group took Touhy's car—the same car used by his hoods when they broke up The Dells casino. Touhy had purchased the car on July 13, 1931 at Marquett Motors at 44 North Larmie Avenue with an initial deposit of $695 and returned later in the day with $2,400 and paid the car off. It was wrongly reported, by Melvin Purvis of the FBI, that the car had a special gas tank to make a ten hour trip. It didn't. But it did have an iron, almost bullet proof sheet that covered its engine block.

Rohrbacher later identified all the Touhys as having stayed at his place in a rented cottage although he was adamant that there were five persons in the party and not four. They had registered under the names of F. McFarland, Chicago; J. Clark, Chicago; Sam Jones, Chicago; E. Davis, Chicago; and Roger as Robert Morgan, Chicago. Robert Morgan was Touhy's father-in-law. Before settling on Rohrbacher's, the group went to the Bayview Cottages, stood on the edge of the lake and then drove away, telling the owner, Al Shape, that they would be back the next day.

They stayed at Rohrbachers Resort for five days and ate all their meals there. According to Rohrbacher, Touhy, sometimes joined by McFadden, did most of the fishing and all of the others told him that it was their first time at the resort area. He said that Sharkey and Schafer were gone in the car most of the day and although they drank enormous amounts of beer "they were agreeable to all other guests at all times" and that they sent back the Milwaukee brand beer he sent up, taking only Hamm's beer telling him that it was the only kind they ever drank.

Walter Kerslake, the Hamm Beer representative for the area, reported selling "many, many cases of beer" to a group of men at Rohrbacher's after George Rohrbacher told him "they were the Touhy gang and had plenty of money and paid for things as they got them."

Rohrbacher remembered Touhy catching a seventeen-pound muskellunge one morning but he gave the fish to another guest, a Doctor Reese of Chicago. An Indian guide named Frank St. Germaine later told the FBI that Touhy went out in the boat fishing alone except on one occasion when he was joined by Schafer. St. Germaine repeated the story frequently that Touhy shot a muskellunge four times before bringing it into the boat and one night at dusk Touhy threw six bottles of beer in the water and fired six shots directly into the necks of all six bottles. Many years later another guide in the region named Jim Ford, said that he had taken Touhy out fishing once and watched as Touhy took a Tommy gun with him to the lake and fired it into the water.

"Tuohy stood up in the boat one day when they

were out fishing and unloaded his Tommy gun on the waters. That old machine gun blasted away. It was good for a laugh. And if I remember, he did get a fish or two."

Fishermen carried pistols to shoot the twenty-five pound muskie because once they were pulled into the boat, they tended to flip around and with their huge, sharp teeth it was better to just shoot them. It was legal to carry a pistol when fishing in those days. However, pistols were outlawed after one too many drunken fishermen shot holes in the bottom of boats or themselves.

On Sunday Touhy, McFadden, Schafer and Sharkey walked into Harry's Place, a saloon run by Harry Bowman and asked for directions to the Minocqua Heights Golf and Country Club.

That testimony was tainted because Bowman had known Eddie McFadden years before. They were also identified by the bartender, Joe Streich. However, the more reliable summer police chief of Minocqua, Jay Jossart, recalled seeing them in the area, as did Deputy Sheriff Titus of Midlake who spotted McFadden at the Chicago Tavern which was owned by Tony Renelli on the southwest side of Lake Delavan. The Touhys had shot and killed Renelli's brother at The Dells two month before.

After Roger and the others were arrested, Renelli told the FBI "that he had heard rumors that he was to be "bumped off" by the Touhys and he appeared to be in great fear. He made the remark during the interview that, "You have the big shots" or "you have the main ones" and that "the others are only barrel pushers for the leaders."

The report went on to say "He also made the remark that the right parties were being held but would not enlarge on the statement and even said that he could not see why Touhy would go into that racket (kidnapping) as he was making good money and also that it was a surprise to him that McFadden would get so involved as he never appeared to be that sort."

Buck Gordon of Gordon's Place, a tavern on the southwest side of Lake Delavan said that he knew Sharkey and that Sharkey had been around there as well. It was Gordon who told Tony Renelli that Sharkey had been around looking for him and had asked Gordon where Renelli was located. Gordon had bought his beer from the Touhys for years. An FBI report read, "He was made to admit that he bought beer from this gang for many years and that regularly once a week, a man would come around to collect. He was shown the photographs of these parties and picked out the photograph of George Wilke as the party who had collected for this beer. He told the story which is not believed by this agent, that he had bought this beer for years but never knew just who he bought from and never questioned the collector or asked for his name. Gordon is known around the region as a braggart."

O.E. Heissler, the manager of the Minocqua Golf and Country Club identified all four of them as having played golf there on two separate occasions but couldn't recall a fifth person, Marshalk, who had been seen with them in most other places around the resort area. After golf, a bathing-suit clad Roger Touhy came into Parker's resort, about mile and half from Rohrbachers. He had arrived in a boat equipped with a Johnson high-powered motor. Parker tried to strike up a conversation with Touhy and said "I know most of the boats on the lake but I can't recall that one, who does it belong to?" He said that Touhy looked at him and asked "What's it to you?" The boat could have belonged to anyone of Touhy's old friends. The area was saturated with bootleggers and other undesirables including Rudy Kreigel, a little known but successful rum runner and Fred Ullrick who ran Ullrick's Resort in Webster, Wisconsin. Ullrick's was a known gangster hideout and suspected by the FBI as being the place where millionaire William Hamm was held during his kidnapping.

Ray Henderson, a bootlegger from Burlington, Wisconsin kept a summer cottage on Lac du Flambeau as did "Bugs" Moran. In fact, Moran's sister, Cassady, lived in the region full time. Sam "Golf Bag" Hunt and Frank Nitti had a place in the north woods, as did Ralph Capone and most of Chicago's mayors. John Dillinger was said to have buried $200,000 in Eagle River and after Jimmy Hoffa disappeared, rumors abounded that Hoffa was buried near a summer place that he owned with Alan Dorfman.

But most important of all, Terrible Tommy O'Connor was said to live in the region where he had been running Touhy's bootlegging operation from a small cabin in Elkhorn, Wisconsin since his disappearance twelve years earlier.

With all of the serious muscle that Touhy had gathered for this retreat, it was clear to everyone that something was afoot. After four days in the lake region, the group left for Chicago on July 19, 1933, a Wednesday morning at about 6:30 A.M. They stopped at Harry Newman's restaurant on Highway 12 near Lake Geneva at 11:00 A.M. and paid their checks separately, each one using clean crisp ten-dollar bills. McFadden purchased the gas with a ten-dollar bill and Touhy wore his alligator slicker that he purchased in Florida in 1931 for "a whole lotta Jack." They stopped for gas once again at Wagner's station just outside of Elkhorn, Wisconsin, where a second car that had been following them waved off, turned around and drove back toward the lakes. It is assumed by many that Terrible Tommy was the second driver.

Elkhorn police officer Harry Ward, a slightly built rookie cop who did motorcycle duty near Highway 12—the road Touhy was using on his way back to Chicago—had just finished his shift and was on his way home when the town bell, an alarm system used to notify police of an incoming call at the station, pierced the air.

Ward answered the call reluctantly. Driving at a high speed, Touhy had knocked over a telephone pole on private property just inside the Elkhorn town line. The owner wanted the car stopped and restitution made for the cost of repairing the damage. The night marshal said, "It's a big Chrysler sedan on Route 12."

Ward stopped Touhy, who was driving seventy miles per hour, because he noticed that the car's left front fender was badly dented. Touhy denied hitting the pole and after a brief, sharp exchange Ward ordered Roger to drive to the police station. It was probably at that point that all of the men in the car slid their guns out of their pockets and into the seat folds. Roy Marshalk, the most wanted of the group, managed to slip out of the car and disappear.

At the police station, Roger was told that the cost of replacing the pole was estimated to be $22. Pay that amount, Roger was told, and he could leave. Roger, who was carrying $2,500 on him, refused to pay, arguing that he had just had placed two phone poles on his property for only $18. An argument broke out that lasted for forty minutes.

Meanwhile, Deputy Ward conducted an illegal search of Touhy's car. Digging his hands deep under the seat cushions he found six pistols, three of them rigged to fire. That was all Ward needed to hold them. Wisconsin was one of the few states to have a law forbidding citizens to carry machine guns, which, technically, the pistol was.

The town Sheriff called Touhy's mortal enemy, Tubbo Gilbert, the States Attorney's Chief Investigator in Cook County. In turn, Gilbert called Melvin Purvis, the FBI's Special Agent in charge of the Chicago office to tell him that Roger Touhy had been arrested in Elkhorn, Wisconsin. Gilbert also said that he felt strongly that Purvis should arrest Touhy for the kidnapping of William Hamm, the St. Paul Brewer who had been snatched off the street several days before.

Purvis agreed, but before leaving for Elkhorn, he held a press conference and declared that "The Touhy gang is being held in Elkhorn by the FBI, where they have positively been identified as being the kidnappers of William A. Hamm."

Roger Touhy had never heard of William Hamm. Nor did he know that several days before his arrest, Hamm had been kidnapped by Alvin Karpis and the Barker gang as he was walking home from his office in St. Paul. Exactly why Karpis decided to kidnap Hamm will probably never be known. Certainly Hamm's wealth was one factor, but there were whispers in St. Paul that while the respectable Hamm's prestigious brewery was selling legal near beer out the front doors, Hamm and the local underworld gang, the Keatings mob, were also selling bootleg beer out the back door.

It was rumored that Hamm, in a moment of stupid ambition or greed or both, double-crossed the

Keatings. The kidnapping and $75,000 ransom it is suspected, was their way of recouping their losses.

Another interesting aspect of the story was that at some point, the Keatings-Hamm operation started to compete with Roger Touhy's own bootleg operation in the Wisconsin area. Threats were made on both sides and tensions ran high. Also interesting was that Roger knew Alvin Karpis. In fact, Karpis had worked for both Al Capone and Frank Nitti as a labor goon in 1930 and 1931, terrorizing and perhaps even killing the same union men that Touhy was being paid to protect. And now Karpis was about to frame Roger Touhy for the Hamm kidnapping. No proof has indicated that the mob ordered Karpis to frame Touhy for the kidnapping, but it seems apparent that they did.

A few days after Hamm was kidnapped his mother died, leaving behind an estate valued at $4,411,647. The public was outraged over her death and blamed the shock of her son's abduction as the cause.

"There was a national hysteria and rightly so against the crime of kidnapping," Touhy wrote. "Clergymen ranted against it from their pulpits and so did editorial writers in their columns. The noisier politicians in Washington tried to outshout each other in being against the crime that everybody loathed...the FBI set up and trained special crews of experts to fly to any section of the country upon a report of a ransom kidnapping. U.S. Attorney General Homer Cummings appointed a special aide, Joseph B. Keenan, to supervise the prosecution of kidnappers. No effort was being spared, or money either, to put an end to kidnapping. Every police officer and prosecutor in America wanted to solve a kidnapping. Anyone of them who put a kidnapper in the electric chair would be a hero. I, Roger Touhy, and two co-defendants were going to have the murky distinction of being the first men convicted."

Eventually, Hamm's ransom was paid and the brewer was released unharmed and Roger Touhy stood accused of the crime.

The day after Roger and the others were arrested, Tubbo Gilbert, Special Agent Melvin Purvis and Chicago Police Chief of Detectives Shoemaker were in Elkhorn to retrieve him. Purvis talked with Touhy first and told him that he was going to be arrested for the kidnapping of William Hamm. "I recalled," Touhy said, "that I had a solid alibi for June 15. I told Purvis so....He looked at me with the tight-lipped, gimlet-eyed way that FBI men had—and which detectives on television have plagiarized."

It made no difference to Purvis. Before noon that day Roger and the others were charged with kidnapping William Hamm and were transported to the FBI's office in Chicago for further questioning. But, back in Chicago, Purvis was worried. None of the money found on Roger or the others could be traced to the William Hamm ransom. Furthermore Purvis knew through informants that Alvin Karpis was the primary suspect in the kidnapping and that Touhy and the others weren't regarded as kidnappers by the underworld or the Chicago police, despite their reputation as gangsters.

"I saw Roger for the first time in person," Purvis wrote, "when he was brought back to Chicago. Handcuffed and under guard, he was delivered to my office. I sat behind my desk and shot questions at him. Touhy wouldn't talk. I can still see him sitting in the leather chair with that mouth full of protruding teeth. His curly hair was neatly barbered, his body was lean and hard under his sports suit, his eyes were dreamy and disarming. Touhy would-n't say a word. When I asked a question he laughed. When I demanded an answer he laughed. Finally I said to him, "Well anyway, what's your name?" Touhy looked at me and grinned, closed his lips and shook his head. He had gained the impression that we were trying to make him talk so an unseen listener might identify his voice as being that one of the kidnappers."

That evening Touhy and others were questioned for hours. While Purvis was in charge, beating prisoners was standard practice for the Chicago office of the FBI. His secretary once wrote, "I sometimes saw the bruised knuckles of the agents who had used more primitive arguments with refractory prisoners."

One so-called refractory prisoner met his death that way. The day after Purvis' agents shot John Dillinger to death, a small time bootlegger named James Probasco was brought to the FBI's 19th floor office in the Bankers Building for questioning. Agents claimed Probasco leaped out of the window for no apparent reason, falling nineteen stories into an alley narrowly missing a passerby. Witnesses later said that the agents held Probasco out the window by his wrists, but lost their grip, causing the outlaw to fall to his death.

In his memos to J. Edgar Hoover in Washington, Purvis said that on this day Touhy was "grilled" by FBI agents from 1:00 P.M. to 5:00 P.M.

Now it was Roger Touhy's turn. "Weeks of hell followed," Touhy wrote. They were kept in isolation in tiny darkened cells. He was allowed to sleep in twenty-minute intervals and then awakened and beaten. The entire processes was repeated twenty minutes later. They punched out seven of his teeth, three vertebrae in his upper spine were fractured and he lost twenty-five pounds in four weeks.

Purvis never did secure a confession out of Roger or the others, but he formally charged them with kidnapping William Hamm anyway.

The following day, as if just to show how bad Roger Touhy's luck could be, President Roosevelt went on national radio and announced the federal government's war on kidnappers.

"The Hamm trial" Roger wrote "had a sort of 'let's pretend we're all nuts' tone to it."

The Department of Justice was so certain of a victory in the case that it asked for the trial to be broadcast live, which would have made it the first ever to go over the airwaves, but the presiding judge declined. However, the government argued successfully that Roger's wife shouldn't be able to testify on his behalf. This was just as well, since the past several weeks had been so hard on Clara.

Purvis, whom Clara had booted off Touhy's estate the week before, had arranged it so that she wasn't allowed into the courtroom until the jury was seated and then she was searched every time she entered the court. When court was over for the day, she retreated to her hotel room, where she clipped newspaper stories about the kidnapping for Roger's lawyer, William Scott Stewart. Lonely and scared, Clara made the mistake of allowing a female reporter into her hotel room to chat. Grateful for the company, Clara spoke freely about anything and everything, including her views on the federal government, the backwoods of Wisconsin, and the jury.

In the next morning's edition, the reporter dramatically twisted virtually everything Clara had said, more or less making her out to be a gun moll and co-conspirator in the case. From that moment on Clara never spoke to another reporter for the rest of her life.

But Clara had a few minor victories as well. When she visited her husband in jail during the trial, two FBI agents dutifully wrote down every word the couple uttered to each other, no matter how commonplace.

Roger recalled:

> Two FBI men, each with a pencil poised above a pad of paper sat at the ends of the table. I smiled at each of them apologetically and said that I hadn't seen my wife for a long time and did they mind very much if I held her hand? They nodded agreeably. Clara and I clasped hands and began telegraphing to each other. A short pressure of a finger was a dot and a long pressure a dash. We had practiced it often when talking secretly in front of our sons. Vocally I talked inanely about our neighbors and such, at the same time telegraphing instructions to her. At the end of our conversation, we coded each other the message of "30" and "73" which meant "that's all" and "Best regards." The listening FBI men gaped at us. They hadn't heard enough to merit putting the pencil to paper.

In court, Roger's lawyer ripped into the government's case and within days had torn it apart. Everything that could go wrong for the government did. The prosecution's primary witness, taxi driver Leo Allison, first positively identified Eddie McFadden as the man who gave him the ransom note and then said it was Roger Touhy. After a drilling by William Scott Stewart, Allison said he couldn't be sure at all.

Another witness who had sworn he overheard ransom demands being made over a pay phone by Touhy changed his tune. On the stand he said

"Roger Touhy bears a close resemblance to the man" he saw and refused to go further. A third witness took the stand and said that he had watched Roger and the others following Hamm in a car as the brewer walked home. Touhy hired private detectives to check the witness out and within two days they were able to prove that this witness had been at work in a printing plant in Chicago on the day he said he saw Touhy and the others in St. Paul. When questioned about why he lied, the witness said that he had been pressured into it by the FBI.

William Hamm couldn't, or wouldn't, identify Touhy and his crew. Instead he appeared extremely evasive on the witness stand. Nor was he any help to the FBI agents who were investigating the case. In fact, right after he was returned by his kidnappers, Hamm flew to New York and stayed there, incommunicado, until the trail began.

Watching their case fall apart, the government started to play hardball. FBI agents went to an Indianapolis hotel where Roger had stayed for one night while Hamm was being abducted. They confiscated the hotel's registration cards and destroyed them.

A key Touhy witness named Edward J. Meany was told by one of Purvis' men "If you go to St. Paul to testify for Touhy, you'll be sorry and maybe you won't come back."

Vincent Connors testified that he had seen Touhy in a night club in Des Plains on the night Hamm was kidnapped. After he gave his testimony he was arrested by the FBI on the dubious charge of registering in a hotel under a false name. Apparently Clara had booked Connors' room under William Scott Stewart's firm's name, which was against the state's moral laws but certainly not a federal offense.

When the trial was over, the United States Deputy Attorney General George F. Sullivan, in his summary of the state's case, mispronounced names, confused dates and lost his place, and when he accused Touhy's lawyer, William Scott Stewart of "vituperative sarcasm and abuse heaped upon the prosecution," Stewart smiled, waved and then took a slight bow.

The jury found them all innocent of kidnapping William Hamm, the first defeat for the government's war on kidnapping since the passage of the Lindbergh law.

Right after they were declared innocent, Willie Sharkey turned to Roger and said "Well, they went through a lot of goddamn trouble for a $22 phone pole." Later that night, Sharkey used his own necktie to hang himself in his cell. Sharkey had shown bizarre behavior for weeks. One time he fell asleep during the trial. When he awoke, he stood up and tried to walk out of the courtroom and had to be pulled back and held down by deputies. Another time, he turned to William Scott Stewart and said in a very loud voice, "My hair is full of electricity, I guess that's a sign," and then laughed uncontrollably for several minutes.

When Touhy was told about Sharkey he said "Willie's life might not have amounted to much, but he shouldn't have been driven to ending it."

As sympathetic as those words were, Sharkey may have feared for his life because during the trial he had talked to the FBI, although no one outside the Bureau is certain of exactly what he told them. Sharkey may have been concerned that FBI agent Purvis[1] told Touhy that he was talking to them—a

1. In 1960, one month after Roger Touhy was murdered, Melvin Purvis, long since retired from the FBI, put a .45 caliber pistol to his head and killed himself.

mean but common trick of the agency.

A day after they were found innocent of kidnapping William Hamm, the Touhys were indicted by the Cook County States Attorney's Office for kidnapping international confidence man John Factor.

Jake The Barber

J ohn Jacob Factor was probably the most successful swindler of all time. He was born Iakow Factrowitz, the second son of a rabbi and the youngest of ten children. Jake, as he preferred to be called, was born in England and taken to Lodz, Poland before his first birthday, where he lived until he was eleven years old. In or about 1900, the family moved to St. Louis, Missouri and then to Chicago.

Although not illiterate, Factor could barely read or write. "I have," he said, "a hazy recollection of several months of schooling in Poland."

It was Factor's mother who supported the desperately poor family through various menial jobs, mostly as a street peddler. Jake's half brother, Max Factor, eventually made his way to California and settled in West Los Angeles. He found work as a make-up artist with the major studios where he helped to create pancake make-up. Pancake is composed of special creams used for Technicolor filming, which kept the actors' faces from appearing green on film. Factor made a few changes to the formula and started to mass market the finished product to department stores, but met with only moderate success. His real success came with the second World War, when the United States Marines ordered massive quantities of his makeup in several shades to use as camouflage.

With money from that order, Max Factor created a product called Long-lasting Lipstick and Water Resistant Mascara, which didn't smear or lose color; his timing could not have been more perfect. The war had pushed women into the work force and they were flush with cash to spend on themselves. As a result, Max Factor Cosmetics became the first successful mass marketed make-up business in America.

Jake Factor took a different route to success. While still a teenager, he went to work as a barber in one of his brother's shops. He used most of the money he earned to support his parents. From that job, Factor picked up the name that would haunt him the rest of his life, a name he hated so much he sometimes paid newspaper people not to use: "Jake the Barber."

Jake left the shop to sell securities in the boom market. He was indicted under a federal warrant for stock fraud in 1919. The case was closed after he returned the funds, only to be indicted again in Florida in 1922 and 1923 for land fraud.[2] There were two more indictments for mail fraud, a gold mine stock swindle in Canada and another in Rhodesia, but the government was never able to obtain a conviction in the cases and Jake the Barber returned to Chicago, rich enough to live in a 14-room apartment on the Gold Coast and employ a

---

2. According to federal documents, the Florida land was sold as "improved lots" when most of the lots were not only unimproved, they were under water.

chauffeur, but still he wanted more.[3]

Sometime in late 1923, Factor convinced New York's master criminal, Arnold Rothstein, to put up an initial cash investment of $50,000 that Factor needed to pull off the largest stock swindle in European history. Handsome, relaxed and likeable, Factor arrived in England in early 1924 and began successfully selling worthless penny stocks.

As it is in any good scam, greed was the hook. Factor assured the investors a guaranteed return of 7 to 12 percent on their initial investments, an enormous sum compared to the one to three percent normally paid out by banks and brokerage houses. Factor was careful about paying each dividend on schedule, but only because it convinced investors to spread the news about their wise investment which brought in even more investors. When enough money was in the till, about 1.5 million, Factor left the country. He left knowing that most of the victims wouldn't file a formal complaint since that would entail revealing both their stupidity and their greed. It proved true. No formal complaint was filed against him.

In early 1925, Factor returned to England, again financed by Rothstein, and planned a second, larger scam. At the heart of the swindle was a stock brokerage firm Factor invented called Tyler Wilson and Company and again, greed was the hook. After offering a carefully compiled list of clients a legitimate stock called Triplex at four dollars a share, Factor, working through the Tyler Wilson name, offered to buy the stock back at six dollars a share, earning his

---

3. Jake was married by then and the father of one child, Jerome. In all Jake would marry three times. In 1925 he married Helen Stoddard who worked at the notorious Freiberg's Dance Hall, one of Chicago's more legendary whorehouses.

victims a quick fifty percent profit.

A month later, Factor, through Tyler Wilson, offered another stock called Edison-Bell, at $3 a share and quickly bought the stock back at $6 a share, careful never to actually deliver the stock certificates to the buyers, meaning that the transaction had only happened on paper. Had the transactions been real, Factor would have lost $750,000.

When the investors were hungry for another deal, Factor sent them another offer for two unlisted stocks named Vulcan Mines and Rhodesian Border Minerals, both of which were supposed to be South African gold mining companies, which Factor hinted, were on the verge of a major expansion. The Barber sold shares in the companies for as low as twenty-five cents each, allowing thousands more to enter the scam, and then pumped the earnings up to as much as $2.50 a share.

It worked. Tens of thousands of money-hungry buyers flooded in, and Jake made sure that each of them got something for their money—an unspecified plot of land in Africa in exchange for their investments—making fraud difficult to prove.

In 1930, England's newspapers started to run articles about Factor and his schemes and there was a persistent rumor that even members of the royal family had invested hundreds of thousands of dollars in his fake stocks. Suddenly, Jake the Barber closed Tyler Wilson and company and fled England with an estimated £1,619,726 or about $8,000,000, an incredible sum of money in 1930. Then, Jake made the one big mistake that would haunt him years later. In December of 1930 he returned to the United States from England, by way of Mexico and up through El Paso, Texas. Factor was admitted back into the United States as a visiting immigrant and swore out a statement that he had been born in Hull, England on October 8, 1892.

The problem was that the United States Immigration Department already had papers on Jake, sworn out by his parents upon their arrival in the States in 1905, that John Factor was a Russian national, born in Lodz, Poland on January 10, 1889. At that point, the immigration service opened an investigatory file on Factor which they would later use to deport him from the country.

New York underworld figure "Legs" Diamond (John Nolan), following Jake the Barber's adventures in England, decided he needed every penny Factor's scam had earned for his narcotics business.

Arnold Rothstein had taught Diamond everything there was to know about the narcotics business, molding him into an expert in heroin imports. Diamond had a knack for the business which in turn made Rothstein, already America's foremost narcotics peddler, a very rich man. But big drug money made Rothstein careless and lazy, which are dangerous traits to have in the volatile world of drug smuggling. Soon others saw the profits from the dope trail that Rothstein had blazed and started to invade his territory. What Rothstein wouldn't give, they took by force.

After Rothstein's death, the remnants of his once vast criminal empire were up for grabs. Diamond quickly laid claim to the European drug importing routes and contacts. But claiming the routes and controlling them were two different things. Command of the U.S. side of the narcotics market hinged on earning money for the European dealers who needed to export their dope into the lucrative and insatiable American market. They wanted to do business with someone who had the cash to flood the

States with low cost, high quality drugs on a continuous basis which would lead to a steady market. Legs Diamond had the money and the connections. Prohibition had made him rich, but all of his cash was tied up in yet another street war over control of bootleg beer outlets. He tried to raise more money to expand the narcotics market from different sources, mostly from the Mafia. But the underworld knew and understood that he lacked any real organizational ability, that he drank too much too often, that he was too violent and far too mentally unstable to deal in the sedate and shadowy world of international drug trafficking.

With nowhere else to turn, Diamond sent word to John Factor over in England that he was taking over all of Rothstein's rackets, including the Factor relationship, and wanted his share of the take from the stock swindles.

Factor never responded, probably assuming that once Arnold Rothstein, his original financier, was dead, that the proceeds from the swindle were his and his alone. But Diamond disagreed, and took a luxury liner to England to find the Barber, but Factor avoided him by simply returning to the United States and hiding out in Chicago, probably cutting in Chicago hoodlum Murray Humpreys for a percentage of his take. Factor knew that a killer like Diamond didn't give up easily, especially when millions were involved, and, never a violent man, Jake the Barber had enough sense to partner with those who had no aversion to violence.

Legs Diamond gave up chasing Jake to attend his own trial in New York State for the attempted murder of a competitor in the bootleg beer business, for which the jury returned a verdict of not guilty. The night after the decision Diamond went out with friends on a drinking binge. He returned to his room in a boarding house in the early morning hours and fell into an alcoholic stupor. A half an hour later, two well-dressed men entered Diamond's room and fired three .38 caliber slugs into his head, killing him.

Murray Humpreys was suspected of engineering the murder, if not committing it himself, on behalf of his new best friend and business partner, Jake Factor but the suspicions were never proven nor was there an investigation into the murder. No one cared. Legs Diamond was dead and that's all that most really wanted.

With Diamond out of the way, Jake the Barber emerged from hiding and when he did, he was arrested in Chicago on the demand of the British government for receiving property knowing it to be fraudulently obtained, but was released on a $50,000 bond.

On December 28, 1931 the United States Commissioner in Chicago ruled that Factor should be extradited to England, where he had already been tried and convicted, *in absentia*, and sentenced to eight years at hard labor. Factor's lawyers appealed on the grounds that each of his victims had received a small plot of land in South Africa, or at least the deed to one, and therefore no one was swindled. A federal judge agreed with Factor and overruled the Commissioner. The Justice Department appealed and the case was headed for the Supreme Court in Washington.

It was generally agreed in legal circles that Factor had a weak case and would be extradited before the spring, but armed with several million in cash and the best lawyers money could buy the Barber managed to delay his hearing until April of 1933.

The Good Son

As usual, Buck Henrichsen, one of Roger Touhy's bodyguards, was having money troubles. A former Cook County Highway patrolman, Henrichsen was a gambler who lost often and lost big; drank too much, and was held in low regard by both Roger and Tommy Touhy.

In April of 1933, Henrichsen and his wife had come to Roger's house and asked Clara Touhy for help. They had fallen behind on all of their payments and their furniture was about to be repossessed. Clara was always more approachable about money than Roger was and after hearing the Henrichsens out, Clara told Roger to pay off their furniture bills, a total of $300, which he did.

Perhaps, thinking that he was now one of Roger's confidants, Henrichsen approached Roger and Tommy Touhy, who was still recuperating from his shooting at the hands of Fur Sammons, and said that he had heard that they were involved in some "easy money deals" (meaning the mail robberies) and he wanted to be in on it.

Roger, always careful, told Henrichsen, "If you

137

know where there's easy money to be made, let me know because I'd like to get in on it."

Henrichsen was insulted and later that day told George Wilke, Touhy's business manager, that there was "easy money being made by the Touhys, but we ain't never going to see none of that. We risk our lives for these people, but we don't never get near the big money."

Wilke agreed. He, Henrichsen and Jim Wagner, who was Touhy's bookkeeper, began to meet privately and talked about ways to make money with or without Roger Touhy.

It was at that point that John Factor came to their attention. Of course Factor wasn't hard to miss. He lived the good life with his stolen loot. He and his wife were seen in the smartest restaurants, chauffeured around Chicago in a silver and gold Deusenberg that cost more then most Chicagoans would earn in a lifetime. He lived in a roof-top bungalow at the Morrison Hotel where he also rented several suites as well as six additional rooms that he used as offices for $1,000 a week. He did all of this at a time when the national income was $6,500 a year and one out of every three Americans was unemployed. Jake's wife—his second—was living at another set of suites at the Hotel Pearson with their six-year-old son Alvin and as always, Jake was supporting his mother and father and relatives in Poland.

The newspaper reported that between his land deal in Florida and his stock scams in England, Jake the Barber had a net worth of at least $20,000,000 and although his actual wealth was probably a fraction of that amount, Jake never denied it.

Buck Henrichsen told the others that he had

checked and as far as he could determine, Jake the Barber wasn't connected to anyone—not to the Touhys or the syndicate. In the psychology of the small time operator like Henrichsen he was fair game and so was the Factor family.

Two days before Factor was due to appear before the Supreme Court, his elder son, Jerome, was kidnapped off the streets of Chicago. A ransom note arrived asking for $50,000 and Murray Humpreys the syndicate labor plunderer and Jake the Barber's close friend was heading private negotiations with the kidnappers from a suite adjoining Factor's.

Humpreys' role in the kidnapping would have gone unnoticed but the messenger who delivered the ransom note was hauled into the police station for questioning and grilled for forty-five minutes.

When he was released, the young man was swarmed by news reporters, "I can't talk to you guys," he said, "Murray Humpreys told me to keep my mouth shut."

Chicago police, incensed at being left out of the investigation, raided a suite at the Congress Hotel, the site of what the press dubbed "the hoodlum detective agency" and arrested a virtual who's who of organized crime in 1933: Murray Humpreys, Machine Gun Jack McGurn, Sam Hunt, Tony Accardo, Frankie Rio, Phil D'Andrea, Rocco DeGrazio and a half dozen other mob bigwigs, all of whom told the police the same story; they were there because they had been brought in by Murray Humpreys to secure Jerome Factor's safe return.

The cops locked them all up on vagrancy charges, but within an hour Factor posted their bail and they were released. While the police were in the apartment, they found a ransom note from Jerome's kidnappers. When questioned, Factor claimed that he had written the note "to confuse the kidnappers."

After eight days of being held hostage, Jerome Factor was released unharmed on a Chicago street. Many people in Chicago simply assumed that Jerome, the good son, had agreed to a kidnapping rigged by his father and Murray Humpreys, to delay the Supreme Court hearing, which it did. However, interestingly enough that same week Buck Henrichsen left Roger Touhy's operation, and he and Jim Wagner opened their own saloons. George Wilke, flush with cash, moved to Florida.

With Jerome Factor returned home safely, John Factor's obligation to appear before the United States Supreme Court was back on schedule.

Factor was an exceptionally smart and practical man. He knew no matter how many shrewd lawyers he could buy with his illegal wealth, that he was going to lose his case before the court and be deported.

Perhaps while discussing his limited options with his attorneys, Factor may have mentioned the delay in the hearing brought about by Jerome's kidnapping. If he, Jake, were kidnapped and then returned safely and his kidnappers were captured, then the ensuing trial would delay his hearings long enough for the statute of limitations against him to run out. It wasn't a sure thing but unless drastic measures were taken his deportation to a jail cell in England, was.

Factor probably brought the idea to Murray Humpreys first, who brought the idea to his boss, Frank Nitti, who liked it. Humpreys and Nitti, and probably Paul Ricca, Nitti's lead counsel in the mob, may have already had information that Jerome's kidnapping had been pulled off by independents who were employed by Roger Touhy.

The shrewd and calculating Ricca was probably the one who decided they would blame Roger for Jake's kidnapping. After all, the mob wasn't having any luck shooting Touhy, or blowing him up, which they had tried several times in the past year. But framing Roger for a kidnapping might work, so Nitti gave his approval with the understanding that none of the syndicate's own people were to be involved. Kidnapping without a long-term purpose wasn't what the mob did; they were racketeers. Kidnapping was a separate profession, a high profile crime that brought in the headline-loving FBI.

The underworld is a small place where news travels quickly. Humpreys learned—probably through Sam Hare, owner of The Dells casino out in the country near Des Plains—that two of Roger's men, Henrichsen and Wilke, not only were behind the Jerome Factor kidnapping, but had pulled it off without Touhy's permission or knowledge.

After that, Humprey, may have approached Henrichsen himself or he may have had him brought to Chicago at gun point. Whichever way he got there, Humpreys threatened to tell Roger Touhy that Henrichsen was behind Jerome Factor's kidnapping. The alternative was for Humpreys to arrange for the Cook County State Attorney's Office to indict Henrichsen and Touhy for kidnapping.

One way or the other, the Touhys would seek revenge and if they didn't, the mob would. It was mandatory. Jake the Barber and his family were under Humpreys' protection, when Henrichsen snatched Jerome. He made Humpreys lose face, so Humpreys had, in the underworld anyway, a legitimate claim to eliminate him. Those were the rules and Henrichsen knew it.

However, always the master deal maker,

Humpreys offered Henrichsen another choice; Jake the Barber wanted to kidnap himself and the syndicate wanted Roger Touhy to take the fall for the kidnapping. If Henrichsen helped them arrange for Jake's disappearance and make it look like a kidnapping pulled off by Roger Touhy, not only would Henrichsen get to live: He could earn some easy money for himself.

Of course Henrichsen agreed to go along with the scheme. It was agreed that Factor would pay $70,000 to fake his kidnapping. With that money, Henrichsen would hire at least nine of Roger's men to work on the scam.

They would fake the kidnapping, hold Factor in a safe house for two weeks, cater to his needs, and then release him safely back to the streets of Chicago where he would accuse Roger Touhy of kidnapping him.

The Hoax

On the afternoon of June 30, 1933 Buck Henrichsen called one of Roger Touhy's former bodyguards, Eddie Schwabauer. Like Henrichsen, Schwabauer had a drinking and gambling problem. However, Schwabauer's habits were so severe that they caused him to be fired by Roger several weeks earlier for being drunk at work.

Henrichsen reached Schwabauer at his mother's house where he was living with his children (his wife having left him a few months before) and told him "a guy with money, a rich guy...needs to disappear for a while. You interested? There's money in it for you."

Schwabauer, who was perpetually broke, said he was interested...very interested. Henrichsen asked if he could put Factor up at Schwabauer's mother's house for a few days and Schwabauer said "Sure, why not?" Before they parted, Henrichsen told Schwabauer to be sure and not say anything to Roger Touhy about it.

Later that same night Jake the Barber and a party of seven, including his wife and his son Jerome, spent the evening in a casino, The Dells, the same place where Roger's men had murdered a syndicate hood a few months before. Factor and his guests drank and gambled until about 1:00 A.M., then piled into Jake's Deusenberg to return to Chicago. As they drove down a narrow, darkened stretch of road, two cars roared up behind them and forced Factor's Deusenberg off the road.

Buck Henrichsen, Eddie Schwabauer, Jimmy Tribbles and "Ice Wagon" Conners—all Touhy men—surrounded Factor's car. With their guns drawn, they dragged Factor from the Deusenberg, tossed him into one of the waiting cars and sped away. An hour later Jake arrived safely at the house of Eddie Schwabauer's mother, where he issued some orders to Henrichsen to get in touch with his family in Chicago and then asked Schwabauer's mother to leave the kitchen while he made several phone calls. Afterward he asked for something to eat and then went to bed about 5:00 A.M.

The next morning, Schwabauer's mother went shopping and saw Factor's picture on the front page of several newspapers. The headlines screamed that Factor had been kidnapped at gunpoint while the British government's representative in Chicago was calling it all a hoax. Outraged and scared, she rushed home and went into her son's room and shook him awake "You tell that Buck Henrichsen that I want that man out of this house. I won't have any part of this!"

An hour later, Henrichsen came to the house with Ice Wagon Connors. They collected Factor and drove him to a rented house in Bangs Lake, Illinois, where Henrichsen and several other Touhy gunmen took turns keeping Factor company. When Jake tired of them, Henrichsen hired the comedic vaude-ville team of Harry Geils and Frankie Brown to

144

Roger Touhy in his cell at the Stateville Penitentiary.
(Photo by Art Shay)

John "Jake the Barber" Factor after serving 6 of his 10 year sentence for mail fraud. (AP/Worldwide)

The King of Crime: Al
Capone.
(AP/Worldwide)

Frank Nitti, the "Enforcer."
(Photo courtesy of the Chicago
Police Department)

Roger Touhy's former business partner and arch enemy, Rocco DeGrazio. (Photo courtesy of the F.B.I.)

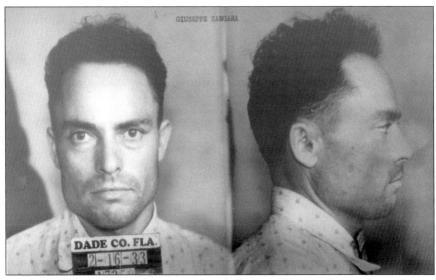

Giuseppe Zangara, the assassin of Chicago Mayor Anton Cermak. (Photo courtesy of the U.S. Secret Service)

On trial for the kidnapping of brewery millionaire William Hamm. Touhy is second from the right. His lawyer, William Stewart, is sitting to his left. (AP/Worldwide)

Barely one month after being cleared of the Hamm charges, the four were arrestd for the kidnapping of John Factor. Left to right: Albi Kator, Edward MacFadden, Gustave Shafer, and Roger Touhy. (AP/Worldwide)

Murray Humphries after being arrested in 1958.
(Photo courtesy of the F.B.I.)

Chicago's Daniel A. "Tubbo" Gilbert, chief investigator and Roger Touhy's nemesis. (Photo courtesy
of the State of Illinois Archives)

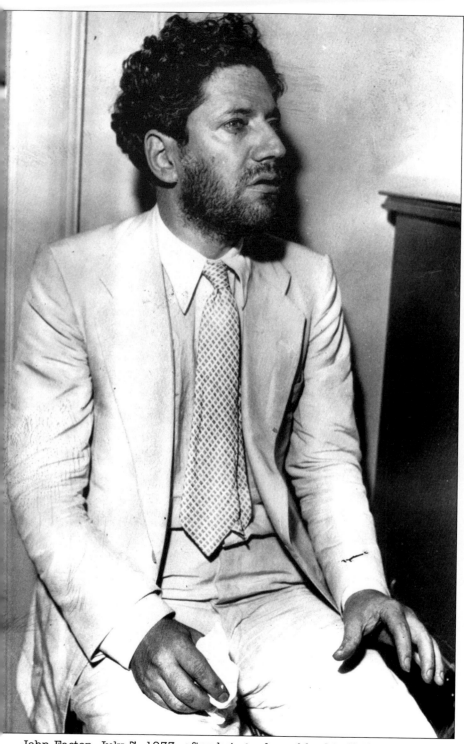

John Factor, July 7, 1933, after being released by his "kidnappers".
(AP/Worldwide)

Max Factor, the founder of the widely successful cosmetics company. He was John Factor's half-brother. (National Archives)

Porky Dillon, (center) and other Touhy gang members
paid to take part in the kidnapping.
(Photo courtesy of the F.B.I.)

The cellar in the Bangs Lake house where Factor claimed he was first held after the abduction. (Photo courtesy of the F.B.I.)

Issac Costner, a major witness against Touhy in the Factor trial. (Photo courtesy of the F.B.I.)

Ludwig "Dutch" Schmidt, who ran the Touhy's mail robbery branch. Schmidt was one of the men John Factor paid to fake his own kidnapping in 1933. Schmidt, however refused to testify against Touhy. He was jailed on the mail robbery charges and died in Atlanta federal prison in 1960. (Photo courtesy of the F.B.I.)

Preston Foster as Roger Touhy (driving) and Victor McLaglen as Basil Banghart in the 1948 film *Roger Touhy, Gangster*. (20th Century Fox, Seven Arts release)

The prison break: Preston Foster (right) with Anthony Quinn in the 1948 film. (20th Century Fox, Seven Arts release)

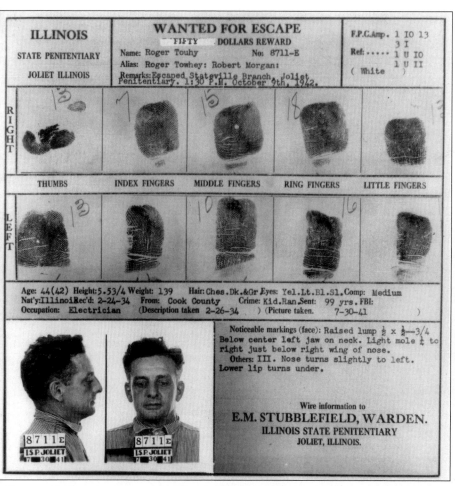

The wanted poster issued by Illinois State Penitentiary for the capture of Touhy. October 9, 1942. (Photo courtesy of the F.B.I.)

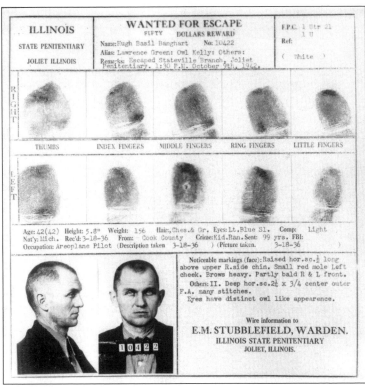

Touhy's confederate in the escape, Basil Banghart. Wanted
poster October 9, 1942.
(Photo courtesy of the F.B.I.)

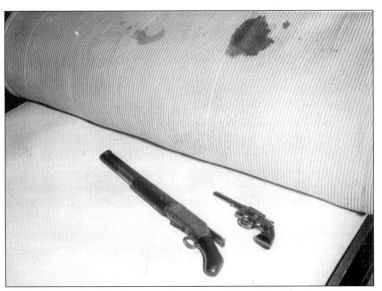

Shotgun and pistol found under Basil Banghart's mattress in
the Touhy hideout. (Photo courtesy of the F.B.I.)

Basil Banghart in 1928. He escaped from Atlanta prison several
days after this photo was taken.
(Photo courtesy of the F.B.I.)

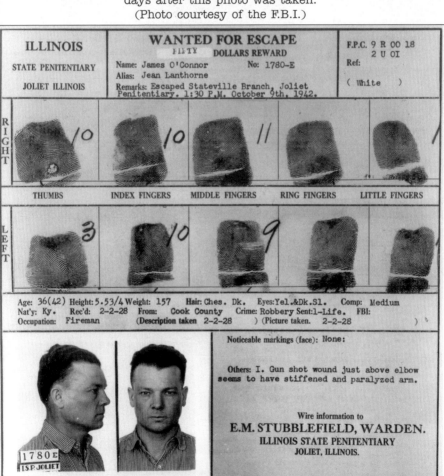

Wanted poster for James O'Connor, October 9, 1942.
(Photo courtesy of the F.B.I.)

Escapees O'Connor and McInerney: killed in the stairway of Touhy's hide-out. (Photo courtesy of the F.B.I.)

With his lawyer, Robert Johnstone,
Touhy is temporarily freed from
prison. August 9, 1954.
(AP/Worldwide)

After a quarter century of incarceration Touhy is
paroled. He is pictured here embracing his wife, Clara.
(AP/Worldwide)

Ambushed in front of his sister's Chicago home, Touhy lies mortally wound-
ed after less than three weeks of freedom. (AP/Worldwide)

entertain Jake who spent the rest of his free time drinking and playing cards.

On July 12, 1933, Jake the Barber Factor showed up in La Grange, Illinois, flagged down a passing police car and announced, "I'm Jake Factor, I was kidnapped!"

Framing Roger Touhy for the kidnapping began the very day that Jake the Barber reappeared. The Chicago newspapers were already quoting Captain Daniel Tubbo Gilbert, the powerful and notoriously corrupt chief investigator for the Cook County States Attorney's Office who, without evidence was already accusing the Touhy gang of having kidnapped Factor.

Gilbert's accusation didn't surprise Roger Touhy in the least; he knew Gilbert hated him. At one time, Gilbert, who was slightly older than Roger, had been close friends with Tommy Touhy. Gilbert and Tommy had known each other since their childhood in the Valley. There Gilbert's upbringing was just as harsh as Tommy's. At age eleven, Gilbert left grammar school and went to work as a wagon-boy at the train depot that once dominated the Valley's center. Within a few years, Gilbert was elected Secretary of the Baggage and Parcel Delivery Union, local 725, when his opponent in the race withdrew after being shot between the legs in mid-election.

Ambitious, Gilbert went on to the governing council of the Chicago Teamsters Union and was then appointed to the Chicago police force on the day the United States entered the first World War. While on the force, Gilbert pursued a separate career in union politics, keeping his position as the Secretary Treasurer of the Baggage and Parcel Drivers Union which he ruled by brute force, fear and intimidation.

During one strike, called by the membership without his authority, Gilbert was so enraged he beat the strike leader so badly that he was indicted for assault with intent to kill. The indictment was later suspended with leave to reinstate. Mysteriously though the records disappeared from the criminal courts building when the Kefauver committee arrived in Chicago in 1951.

On the force, Tubbo earned a reputation as a cop on the make, a thick-necked bully, quick with his fist. He rose through the ranks with lightning speed because he openly engaged in city politics. He was smart enough to surround himself with capable and bright underlings. But in 1923 Gilbert was still a beat cop supplementing his income by shaking down small time bootleggers like Roger Touhy.

One afternoon Gilbert called Roger into the station and told him he wanted $5 for every barrel that rolled through his district even if it was near beer, because the city's biggest bootlegger, Johnny Torrio, had his breweries closed by federal order. As a result, payoff money had gotten tight. Roger told Gilbert that he assumed his friendship with his brother Tommy had taken care of finances but Gilbert made it clear that friendship and money were two different issues.

Roger, as cocky as ever, told Gilbert that he expected to pay for protection but that Gilbert's asking price was exorbitant since a single barrel cost Roger $12. If he had to pay Gilbert $5 on every barrel plus an additional $5 to his drivers, then he would have to go out of business. Gilbert held tight to his asking price and Roger refused to budge, so Gilbert had all of his trucks impounded. Roger walked over to the 27th Ward Democratic Club where he knew he would find Gilbert, and told him that the trucks he impounded were loaded with near beer and therefore legal, and that he wanted the trucks released.

Gilbert said he didn't care if it was near beer or the real thing. He wanted $5 a barrel to release the trucks but again Roger refused to pay and, being on the right side of the law for once, threatened to take his complaint to Gilbert's superiors.

Gilbert relented and accompanied Roger back to the police impound yard and while others watched and listened, Gilbert made a loud apology for what he termed "this unfortunate oversight" and assigned several policemen to reload the trucks. When the trucks were reloaded, Gilbert pulled Roger aside, his face red with fury, and said, "I don't care what kind of beer comes into this district it's a fin a barrel or no beer comes into the district at all."

Roger told Gilbert he would pay $1.50 a barrel for protection, the going rate, and that was all that he would pay. The argument went around and around and for the next six months. Gilbert continued to stop every Touhy truck that he could find and Touhy still refused to pay. Thus the lifelong feud between Tubbo Gilbert and Roger Touhy continued.

Now, in 1933, Tubbo Gilbert was sitting comfortably in the syndicate's palm and was part of the conspiracy to frame Roger Touhy for John Factor's kidnapping. But, no matter how much Gilbert and the mob tried to build up the kidnapping tale, by the end of the summer of 1933, the story was starting to unravel. As more and more of the seamy details of his criminal career came out in the newspapers, the public was beginning to doubt that Factor had been abducted at all.

As the wall closed in on him, Factor's only choice was to bring the public's sympathies back to his side, while at the same time building a better case against Roger Touhy. Through his contacts within Touhy's gang, Factor was able to get in touch with a Tennessee moonshiner turned mail bandit, Isaac Costner, who was loosely associated with one of Touhy's top men, Basil Hugh Banghart.

Factor told Costner that he had kidnapped himself to avoid extradition and that he needed to build up his story and that he would pay Costner a $25,000 fee to make the kidnapping look real. For this fee Factor insisted Costner would have to bring Basil Banghart into the deal. Costner assured him that he would.

Basil Hugh Banghart had been born in Berryville, Michigan in 1900 and finished one year of college before he became a professional car thief, stealing some 100 autos in Detroit in three months in 1926 before he was arrested and imprisoned. Sociologists rated him as "a professional, sophisticated criminal, who is astute, well poised, alert, but without social conscience or scruples. He used his I.Q. of 117 to learn to drive a train and fly an airplane...and steal cars."

Assigned to a window-washing detail in Atlanta Federal Prison, Banghart made his first escape by leaping some twenty-five feet from a window into a marsh on the other side of the prison's walls. He eventually made his way to Montana, but was re-captured and sent back to Atlanta.

His second escape from Atlanta was with the legendary mail robber Gerald Chapman in 1927, but again, he was re-captured. Banghart was escorted back to prison by a U.S. Marshal with a stop over at the Federal building in Baltimore where Banghart was left in an office alone for several minutes. Banghart used the time to call the local police, telling them he was an FBI agent who had been overpowered and handcuffed by the prisoner he was escorting back to prison, "a dangerous, armed felon and a police imposter" he said. The police rushed to the building, arrested the marshal and released Banghart who was re-captured once again in Knoxville a year later and returned to Atlanta.

He escaped yet again and was arrested in Detroit for armed robbery and was being held in the South Bend, Indiana jail when he escaped one more time by throwing pepper in a guard's face, grabbing his machine gun and shooting his way to freedom. This time Banghart successfully made his way to Chicago and went to work for Roger Touhy as a gunner and mail robber.

Now, in the summer of 1933 Basil Banghart and Isaac Costner met Jake the Barber in suburban Maywood, Illinois to discuss Factor's kidnapping. Banghart was suspicious, so Factor explained that there were too many holes in his kidnapping story and that too many people were starting to doubt the whole thing. The British government wouldn't let up on its demands to have him extradited. He said he was willing to pay them $25,000 in cash if they would call him and demand more money while the FBI and police listened in on the line.

After a few demands from them, Factor said he would arrange a time and place for the additional ransom money, $25,000, to be paid. Then Factor gave Costner $5,000 as a down payment and Banghart agreed to go into the deal. A day later, Costner placed the call to Factor's hotel suite while Tubbo Gilbert and Special Agent Melvin Purvis of the FBI listened in on the call. Costner identified himself as one of the kidnappers and demanded to know when the second half of the ransom would be paid. Factor replied that he was having difficulty raising the money and that Costner should call back in a day or two.

Then, to the absolute horror of police professionals, after the call had ended Factor called a press conference and said that he had received a telephone demand for more money from the kidnappers and that Chief of States Attorney's Investigators Tubbo Gilbert and Special Agent Melvin Purvis were listening in on the line at the time. The papers ran with the story and suddenly Jake the Barber's kidnapping story was credible again.

Eventually Costner and Banghart arranged to pick up the additional ransom on the corner of Wolf and Ogden Roads, just outside the forest preserves.

In preparation, Chicago Chief of Detectives William Shoemaker rounded up 250 heavily armed policemen, police cadets, sheriffs, deputies and FBI agents, two airplanes and sixty-two squad cars, ten machine guns and a dozen drop bombs and then huddled with Melvin Purvis and Tubbo Gilbert for three days to plan the kidnappers' capture.

It had been agreed that the money would be dropped off by a messenger in a taxi cab and the police commandeered a cab that they filled with two officers, armed with machine guns and pistols, drove to the pick up point and waited. Banghart was late picking up the money and sped onto the road where the cab was waiting and pulled up to the taxi's fender, screeching to a halt, just barely avoiding an accident. He stepped out and walked over to the cab and looked at plainclothes officer Patrick McKenna in the back seat.

"You got a package, a package for Smith?" he asked.

McKenna nodded "Yes. It's here." At that,

McKenna climbed out of the car, looked up at the two police airplanes circling above them and waved his arms to signal that the pickup had been made.

Banghart saw the set up, if in fact he hadn't already been told about it by Gilbert, and floored his car down the road only to find it blocked by a dozen squad cars. Throwing the car in reverse, he raced down to the other end of the road to find another road block. He threw the car in reverse again and dodged back and forth between the roadblocks looking for an opening. At one point the two cops in the taxi, McKenna and Meyers, drove up behind Banghart's car and fired a machine gun at the gangster, missing every shot. In frustration, Meyers pulled the cab up alongside Banghart's car to give McKenna a better target. McKenna let a burst go from the Tommy gun but missed again. This time, Banghart drove straight at the roadblock in front of him and the cops, not really sure if he would stop or not, moved out of his way. Banghart drove into the forest preserve to get out of the view of the airplanes above him. With the police only yards behind him, Banghart leaped out of the car, let it smash into a tree and ran away on foot into a rain gully that led to a state highway. From there, he hitchhiked back to Chicago, $25,000 richer, or so he thought. When Banghart opened the package, he found only $500 and stacks of cut up newspapers.

Convicted

R oger Touhy's trial for kidnapping Jake Factor was scheduled for November of 1933.

William Scott Stewart would again be defending Roger and the others. Heading the prosecution's team was Thomas J. Courtney, a tall, handsome Irishman with an easy smile who had recently been swept into office as the Cook County States Attorney in the 1932 Democratic landslide. Courtney was a man with a background. He was a lawman who had operated a speakeasy and book-making joint. He was a man who bought his booze and protection from Frank Nitti just like everyone else in Chicago. Inside Chicago City Hall, Courtney was widely considered something of a bumbler. Though handsome, he was a dim-witted figurehead who was intimidated by the older and tougher Tubbo Gilbert who, although he was supposed to work under Courtney's direction, virtually ran the office. As for Gilbert, to prepare for the Factor kidnapping trial, he bugged Touhy's lawyer's phones and kept them bugged until 1936, well after the trial had ended.

If Tubbo Gilbert was the muscle behind the States Attorney, the brain was a first rate lawyer named Wilbert Francis Crowley, acting as Courtney's first assistant. Unlike Courtney or Gilbert, Crowley wasn't a professional politico with higher political goals or a driving greed. He was a former public defender who was so good at what he did—defeating the States Attorney's Office—that he was offered the position as Courtney's assistant, where he virtually ran the judicial side of the office.

To have a trial, the prosecution would need a victim, so with the assistance of States Attorney Courtney, U.S. Secretary of State Cordull Hull and the Justice Department, Jake Factor's deportation hearing was postponed since he would be needed as a witness for the prosecution. After the hearing was postponed, Factor's image in the press changed for the better, literally, overnight. Reporter Milton Mayer recalled being surprised to read in his paper that Factor was now "John Factor, wealthy speculator."

"I kept filing the story as Jake the Barber but it kept coming out John Factor, wealthy speculator."

Mayer went to see his editor who said that "States Attorney Courtney was up here and he's asked the papers to use the expression 'John Factor, wealthy speculator' so as not to prejudice prospective jurors in the Touhy trial."

Touhy's image in the newspapers suffered. "The stories in the Chicago papers irked me a little," he said. "The news stories now were calling me 'Black Roger' and 'Terrible Touhy.' I discovered that I was a machine gunner, a bomber, a probable murderer and a few other things about myself I didn't know."

The trial was presided over by Michael Feinberg, who had earned a reputation as one of Chicago's least qualified judges. In 1932, Feinberg ran in the

Republican primary against John Swansa for the position of chief judge, but the Chicago Bar Association refused to endorse him, stating "He has used his judicial position to further his campaign for state's attorney. In this he has shown a lack of appreciation of obligations of judicial office." The *Chicago Tribune* went a step further and flatly advised the public against voting for Feinberg at all.

After he lost the primary, Feinberg resigned from the Bar Association and ordered a special grand jury to look into fraud in the elections. The grand jury was disbanded by the Illinois Supreme Court who wrote that Feinberg had no such right to call the jury in the first place and that "he has demonstrated a lack of qualifications essential to the holding of judicial office."

In as far as the Touhy case was concerned, Feinberg saw it as a waste of the taxpayers' money. Touhy was, in Feinberg's eyes, guilty of something; if it wasn't kidnapping John Factor, then it was something else. As Roger wrote, "Feinberg wanted a trial right now—or sooner, if possible. There would be no delays, which left us little time to locate witnesses or prepare a defense."

Several days before the trial began Touhy wrote that "an emissary came to me in the jail with a proposition. A message had been sent to him that [we] would go free for a pay-off of $25,000 to a politician. I said the hell with it. I was innocent and no politician was going to get fat off of me."

Years later, Roger told newsman Ray Brennan that the politician who wanted the kickback was actually Judge Feinberg, and that the reason he refused to pay was that his own sources in City Hall told him that Feinberg had already shaken down Jake Factor for $25,000 assuring him of a conviction.

Jake the Barber was the first witness called to the stand. One of the questions Crowley asked him was if he was allowed to use the bathroom while he was being held captive by Roger Touhy. Factor said that he was.

"And how many times," Crowley asked, "while you were in the basement, did you use the lavatory?"

"Very often, that night," Jake replied.

At that point, Chicken McFadden leaned over to Touhy and said in a voice loud enough for the jury to hear, "He's trying to get it across that Jake had the shit scared out of him."

Factor said that right after he was kidnapped, he was blindfolded and tied, brought to a house and walked down to a basement where he was tied to a wooden chair. He said he could sense "several men around me, a single light bulb burning over my head."

He said that the kidnappers demanded that he give them the name of a person he could trust as a contact and Factor said he suggested Joe Silvers or Sam Hare, owners of The Dells, where Factor had been gambling just before he was kidnapped.

But Joe Silvers would never get to testify and Factor probably knew that when he gave his name from the witness stand. Silvers was facing federal charges for mail robbery and decided to turn informant rather than do time. Perhaps fearing that he would tell what he knew about the Factor disappearance, Murray Humpreys' boys had followed Silvers down to Florida, kidnapped him, took him out on a boat, shot him and threw him overboard.

Silvers' partner in The Dells, Sam Hare, wouldn't fare much better. Somebody pulled up alongside his car as he was driving along on a Chicago highway and shot him.

Factor went on to say that right after he gave their names as contacts, he was left alone with two men whom he dubbed "the good man" and "the bad man." The bad man was the one who slapped him around, robbed him of his rings and watch and threatened to cut off his ears "and send them to your wife as souvenirs."

However, when he complained that the blindfold around his head was too tight, Factor said that the "good man" removed it from his eyes, cut it into pieces and then pasted it back over his eyes with adhesive tape.

Factor said that while his eyes were uncovered he looked up and saw Roger Touhy whom he now identified as the "bad man."

Factor said that the next day he was told by the bad man "You're going for a ride," and assumed that meant he was going to be killed and wept for his life.

Factor claimed that at this point he was driven to another house. There he was forced to write a ransom note while someone held a machine gun to the back of his head. The ever astute Stewart asked Factor "How did you know it was a machine gun? Do you have eyes in the back of your head?"

Crowley objected to the question and the objection was upheld by Judge Feinberg. "Crowley objected to every question asked of Factor," Touhy said, "and Judge Feinberg upheld the prosecution most of the time."

Despite the judge's apparent predisposition toward the prosecution, Stewart's cross-examination of Factor was brutal and relentless. Though he managed to cause Factor to confuse his story, it was clear he was fighting an uphill battle.

Next, the state called Eddie Schwabauer to the stand. Tubbo Gilbert, of the Cook County States

Attorney's Office, and Jake the Barber had long since gotten to Schwabauer and bribed him to lie on the witness stand, which he did and did well. He testified that on the night Factor was kidnapped he was doing guard duty in Touhy's yard. This wasn't true. Weeks earlier Touhy had fired him for being drunk on duty. Still, Schwabauer said that on the night in question that the Touhy household was uninhabited all night. Schwabauer's testimony directly contradicted Touhy's defense that he had spent most of the night sitting on his front porch with his wife and her girlfriend, Emily Ivins.

Schwabauer's mother, Mrs. Clara Sczech, who according to Touhy was "a poor, middle aged, bedeviled, bewildered woman," testified next. Sczech was a maid in a house in Glenview, Illinois rented in Eddie McFadden's name for one of the union bosses. There, she claimed she saw Basil Banghart and someone who looked like Roger Touhy. Her precise words were, "I'm not sure whether I seen him there or not." Then, pointing at Touhy, a man she had known for at least five years, she said "This here fellow looks quite a lot like him, still there is not quite so much resemblance."

She ended her testimony with a lie, saying that after Factor was released by his kidnappers, McFadden told her that she was no longer needed to clean the house. The implication being that the house was where Factor was held during his kidnapping.

Buck Henrichsen testified next. He appeared completely relaxed, having spent the past seven weeks before the trial living in protective custody at Chicago's finest hotel, the Palmer House, courtesy of the States Attorney.

Roger didn't know anything about Henrichsen's

testimony until the day he took the witness stand. Of this unexpected testimony Touhy wrote, "I didn't expect Buck Henrichsen to shove a knife between my ribs and twist it. I had never done anything but good for him....Henrichsen couldn't meet my eyes when Crowley called him to the witness stand. He was ashamed."

Henrichsen testified that Roger ordered him to find a house in Glenview for Eddie McFadden to rent, and that on the night Factor was kidnapped, he had seen Touhy at Jim Wagner's saloon drinking with Schafer, Kator, Banghart and the others who were now accused of the kidnapping.

His testimony of course was false. Regardless of their validity his words proved to be very damaging to Roger's case. As far as the jury knew Henrichsen was a former police officer and simple night watchman around Roger's home who had no reason to lie about his employer on the witness stand.

After Henrichsen's testimony, Roger demanded that his lawyer, William Scott Stewart, place him on the stand. Stewart refused. This led Roger to sign an affidavit requesting a new lawyer. Insulted, Stewart refused to go on with the trial. Eventually he resumed but only after Judge Feinberg threatened to jail him. When Stewart refused Feinberg's order and simply didn't show up for court the judge sent his bailiff to Stewart's home and escorted him back to the courtroom in handcuffs.

Touhy recalls,

As the trial moved toward a close, I was fed up to the Adam's Apple with our lawyer. So were Kator and (Schafer). Somebody had told me that Stewart had gone to lunch with Crowley and that he had chatted with Tubbo Gilbert during a court recess....Stewart, although he knew I was innocent, wouldn't listen to me...the squabbling between us was endless.

His fate was now in the hands of a man he didn't trust.

After three weeks of testimony, the jury retired. After only one day's deliberation the trial was dismissed by Judge Feinberg as deadlocked. A second trial was to begin in eleven days.

The second trial was almost a duplicate of the first. The only exception was the testimony of Ike Costner and Basil Banghart whom Factor called to build up his story.

Costner's testimony was part of a deal he made following his arrest in Baltimore in February of 1933 along with Basil Banghart for their part in a $105,000 mail truck robbery in Charlotte, North Carolina.

Upon learning of Costner and Banghart's arrest, Tubbo Gilbert, Jake Factor and six deputies traveled by train to Maryland. Also joining them was Joseph P. Keenan, the Special U.S. Attorney charged by the Attorney General with stopping the rash of kidnappings that were plaguing the country. With Keenan's help, Costner and Banghart were released in Gilbert's custody and somewhere along the train ride back to Chicago, Ike Costner agreed to lie on the witness stand in return for a lighter sentence in the mail robbery case.

"On the day that Factor and Gilbert brought the two witnesses back from Baltimore," Touhy wrote, "I was walking in the corridor leading from Judge Feinberg's courtroom to the prisoner's elevator during a recess. Ahead of me, I spotted Tubbo Gilbert and a man I never had seen before. I figured it might be another fake finger, so I hunched down my head and hid my face with my coat collar. I heard Tubbo say 'The guy in the light suit, that's Touhy'...in my cell, I got the hell out of that light suit and put on a dark blue one. When I got back to the court, Costner was the first witness."

Crowley asked Costner "And did you know Roger Touhy?"

Costner went blank and didn't answer. Crowley asked again and Costner mumbled "Yes."

"Please point to Mr. Touhy. He is present in the courtroom."

Costner looked around the room desperately. He didn't have a clue as to what Roger Touhy looked like.

Ray Brennan, who covered parts of the trial for the Associated Press, later said that Costner looked over at the defense table and stared at one of the Cook County deputies guarding the Touhys and was about to point to him as the man he suspected of being Roger when Stewart said very loudly, "Stand up, Roger."

Touhy was mortified but stood up, expressionless.

"Yeah, that's him," said a relieved Costner.

"Did you know Gus Schafer?" Crowley continued.

Again Costner went blank and again, remarkably, Stewart shouted "Stand up Gus," and Schafer stood up, a look of complete disbelief on his face.

"Did you know Kator? Albert Kator?" Crowley asked.

Stewart told Kator to stand which he did.

Crowley asked Costner if he saw all three men at the apartment house and Costner said he had seen them there.

"I have always been bitter," Roger wrote, "and always will be about Stewart's making me a clay pigeon for Costner to shoot down....Stewart said he regarded it as psychologically important with the jury to have a defendant admit his identity at once, rather than wait to be pointed out. Maybe so, but I don't believe Costner could have identified me without my own lawyer's help."

Costner testified that he had come to Chicago at Basil Banghart's request because Banghart was eager to get money for Touhy's defense in St. Paul against the Hamm kidnapping charges.

Stewart leaped to his feet and shouted "What! What lawyer?"

"I don't remember, Banghart never told me his name."

Costner said that it was Touhy's enforcer James Tribbles who pulled him into the Factor kidnapping in the first place.

It was safe to accuse Tribbles because he was dead. They found him almost the same way they found Teddy Newberry, tied with chicken wire, beaten to a purple pulp and shot in the head and dumped alongside a ditch. Everybody blamed Tommy Touhy for the murder, but by then Tommy's legs had given out and he was confined to bed in a log cabin hidden away on Joe Saltis' estate in rural Wisconsin.

Costner said that on the night Factor was kidnapped, Tribbles took him to a lonely, rural side road near The Dells where Roger Touhy, Kator, Schafer and Banghart were waiting. When Factor pulled out of The Dells' parking lot, Costner said that the club owner, Joe Silvers "put the finger on Factor."

Costner went on to admit that he was "the good man" that Factor had spoken of during his testimony.

When called to the witness stand again to face a

grilling by William Scott Stewart, Costner was made to look like the liar that he was. His eyes darted from left to right and he rubbed his hands together and perspired profusely.

Stewart asked Costner for the address of the apartment house in which he lived but he said he couldn't remember what it was.

"Ok, can you tell us what city or town place it was in?"

"No, I forget."

"So you don't know the address, or street name or city name of the place where you lived for eighteen months, is that correct?"

"I think it is." Costner said.

To the rest of Stewart's questions Costner's replies were similar. His refrain was "I don't know," and "I don't recall right at this moment."

When Basil Banghart was called to the stand, Crowley asked,

"What is your occupation, Mr. Banghart?"

"Thief."

The jury laughed but Crowley was confused.

"What?"

"I'm a thief. I steal...that's how I make my living."

"And you're proud of that?"

"Why not? You're a lawyer, lots of people say you people steal, I don't hear you apologizing to nobody."

"I am not on trial here, sir."

"Well, neither am I, son."

"What was the last place of your residence?"

"601 McDonough Boulevard South East, Atlanta, Georgia, but it wasn't permanent."

Later in the day Crowley found out that 601 McDonough was the address for the Atlanta Federal prison and called Banghart back to the witness stand to explain himself.

"Why didn't you tell us," Crowley demanded, "that you were in prison?"

"Four walls and iron bars," Banghart replied, "do not a prison make."

Crowley said, "So you escaped from prison, isn't that correct?"

Banghart answered, "No. The warden says I escaped from prison."

"And," Crowley asked, "What do you say?"

"I say," replied Banghart, "that I left without permission."

"The point is, Mr. Banghart, is that you are a fugitive, are you not?"

"Yes I am. I am a fugitive."

"From where?"

"From justice."

Despite the fact that the only new testimony was shaky at best, the jury took less than four hours to decide their guilt and six hours to decide the penalty. Half the jurors wanted to impose the death penalty and half wanted life in prison. Ultimately Roger was sentenced to ninety-nine years in Joliet State Prison.

When the verdict was read, Roger gagged, coughed violently, vomited, and had to be carried out by deputies while the courtroom exploded in cheers.

In a separate trial, Isaac Costner and Basil Banghart were also found guilty for their role in the Factor kidnapping and given ninety-nine years each. Costner screamed double-cross and said that the federal government promised to let him off with five years if he testified against the Touhys in the Factor case. The government denied any such promise, saying that they had no interest in making deals for the Cook County States Attorney's Office.

The day Roger Touhy went to prison, the syndicate, led by Rocco DeGrazio, moved into his section of Cook County and never moved out again.

Now that Roger and the others were convicted, John Factor had a problem; he was going to be extradited, or so he thought.

But the U.S. Department of State made no moves to extradite him and Factor was free. He had beaten deportation. However, the conviction against him by the English courts was ordered to remain in effect until he was tried before a Royal Bench in England and that day would come sooner than he or anyone else realized.

The Private Detective

D espite his conviction, Touhy was not giving up his fight. From prison, in 1938, Roger retained Thomas Marshall as counsel with his last $50,000. Marshall was one of the nation's leading criminal lawyers. After sifting through the evidence, Marshall was convinced of Roger's innocence, but decided that what was needed was a complete reinvestigation of the case. With Touhy's approval, Marshal brought in a private detective named Morrie Green, a disbarred lawyer who had once represented most of the Chicago underworld, including the Moran Gang's leader, Schemer Drucci. Green had also been the lawyer for super pimp and political pay-off expert Jake Zuta. In fact in that case, Green may have overstepped the fine line between lawyer and partner when Green's signature was found on several checks written from Jake Zuta to himself, and then signed over to a judge Joseph Schulman of the municipal bench. The judge said that he had business dealings with Morrie Green and that was why Zuta had the checks. Disbarred, Green spent the last part of his career as a private detective.

• • •

An interesting note on Green—in 1959, long after the Touhy case, he would make the newspapers again when the underworld murdered Fred Evans. Evans and Murray Humpreys had started their criminal careers together back in the Roaring Twenties and by 1959 both of them were powerful men. Evans' loan-sharking operation eventually put him in touch with Lou Greenberg, a lowlife character who ran Capone's Manhattan brewery and the Roosevelt Finance Company at 3159 Roosevelt Road. Greenberg had his life snuffed out after he cheated Frank Nitti's adopted son out of his inheritance which Greenberg had been entrusted to hold until the boy came of age. Eventually Evans and Greenberg's widow, Esther, would become partners in a luxury hotel in Beverly Hills. Coincidentally, it was at that hotel in 1951 that wise guys from Chicago and St. Paul planned the execution of a Los Angeles reform mayor. Eventually the two made enough money to reinvest their profits into another hotel just inside Beverly Hills.

By 1959 Evans was a rich man. His fortune was at least eleven million dollars in cash. Most of that was made in the early 1940s when Evans worked the inroads that Humpreys and Teddy Newberry had made in their brokerage firm shakedown schemes in the late 1930s. With Humpreys' muscle behind him, Evans ended up with part ownership of a discount brokerage corporation at 100 North La Salle Street in Chicago. By now Evans was considered to be the brains behind Humpreys' financial success and was widely thought to be the fiscal genius behind Frank Nitti's ability to wash the extortion money from Hollywood's Bioff scandal.

The FBI made a customary stop at Evans' office and briefly interviewed him. He consented to answer questions, but was guarded in his conversation. While speaking with Evans, the agents weeded through a pile of useless information to find out that Morrie Green was a front for Humpreys in the Superior Laundry and Linen Supply Company which he owned lock, stock and barrel.

It seemed, to Evans anyway, to be a fairly worthless piece of information—most law enforcement people and wise guys in Chicago already understood the relationship between Humpreys and Greenberg. However the FBI didn't know it. In fact in 1959 the FBI knew very little about organized crime.

The agents took what they learned from Evans and confronted Morrie Green with the information and its source. Word got back to Ricca and Accardo and Giancana that Evans had talked to the federal government.

The bosses sat in judgement with the evidence before them and decided that Evans had to be eliminated. It didn't matter what he had said; the fact was that he had communicated with the FBI. As a courtesy to Humpreys, since he and Evans went back so far, the boys asked if the Hump could come up with a reason not to kill Evans. Humpreys shrugged and said he had nothing to say on the subject. That sealed Evans' fate.

Twenty-one days later, on August 22, 1959, Fred Evans finished up work at his desk. He had been going over his assets. Closing his books he scribbled "total resources eleven million dollars" on a paper which he left in the middle of his desk. He turned off his desk lights and left the office, walked to 5409 West Lake Drive, where his Cadillac was parked at a lot. As Evans walked across the lot, Mrs. Alice Griesemer of 328 North Lotus Avenue, saw a young man wearing a heavy winter coat, buttoned to the neck, who had been sitting on a step for over an hour on an extremely muggy Chicago evening. As Evans strolled in front of Mrs. Griesemer's line of vision the young man in the winter coat leaped to his feet and ran across the street into the parking lot towards Evans. At the same time, another man holding a handkerchief across the lower part of his face ran out of an alley toward Evans. It took Evans and Mrs. Griesemer only a few seconds to see that both of the men had pistols in their hands. Evans stopped in his tracks and covered his face and yelled "No, don't!"

The two men slammed Evans against a wall, searched him quickly and snatched an envelope from his back trouser pocket. Leaping backward they shot him twice in the head and twice in the throat. The shots in the throat were to let the underworld know that they suspected Evans of being a stool pigeon.

The assailants leaped into a blue Chevrolet and vanished.

Evans staggered a few feet back to his car and collapsed across the front seat. The witness, Mrs. Griesemer, on North Lotus Avenue, said "It was like watching a movie or a television show."

When the police arrived they found Evans' body lying on an envelope that held a $5000 government bond. Further investigation of the contents on Evans' desk showed that he held about $500,000 in cash, jewelry, stocks and bonds and part ownership of two apartment buildings. In the end he paid the ultimate price for committing the underworld's one mortal sin—talking to the feds. It didn't matter that the information he divulged about Morrie Green's relationship with Murray Humpreys was old news to most; Evans sealed his fate by talking at all.

• • •

In the last months of 1938, before becoming embroiled in the Evans shooting, Morrie Green was working as a private investigator for Roger Touhy. There's no doubt that the two men had known each other on the outside. Chicago's underworld was too small for them not to have known each other. "Morris," Roger said, "seemed a bit cynical when he first came to see me. He sat across the visitor's table in the long, narrow room where fifty or more convicts can talk with their lawyers or with their relatives on approved visiting days. I could see that Green wasn't happy with his mission." However, "Green surprised me," Roger said. "He was a jewel, a really rich prize....Morrie turned out not to be really a cynic. He was a kind, considerate, conscientious man...who had bitter disappointments in his life, and he had an understanding for informants like me. People expect to be bled white by private detectives. Although my legal expenses had been enormous, I still had about $50,000 which my family had salvaged from my ruined beer business. But Green charged only reasonable fees and he didn't pad his expense account."

The first thing Green did was visit Buck Henrichsen, Touhy's former bodyguard. With Touhy in prison, Henrichsen found full time work for himself with Chicago's gambling czar, Billy Skidmore, at the mob's Bon Aire Country Club. The Bon Aire wasn't actually a country club at all. It was a posh casino owned by the underworld—mostly by Tony Accardo—and run by Skidmore, the syndicate's favorite front man. Each weekend buses owned by the mob delivered hundreds of gamblers to the club. Somehow, despite the casino's high profile, it was never raided.

The fact that Henrichsen was working for Billy Skidmore was no small thing either. Roger had known Skidmore from his childhood when Skidmore ran a notorious saloon on West Lake and North Robey streets[4] only a few doors down from the house where Roger had been born. Confidence men and petty criminals gathered at the saloon to divide their spoils, and gamblers and pimps arrived to pay their protection money. The place also served as headquarters for Valley pickpockets, sneak thieves and shoplifters of all sorts. Skidmore sold bail bonds to them all. But what Skidmore did best was to act as a go-between—firming up deals between gangsters and politicians—ultimately serving as the bag man when a deal was worked out.

Otherwise, Skidmore was a hustler. He ran gambling joints inside the Levee and was a regular visitor to Johnny Torrio's Four Deuces saloon at 2222 South Wabash. In 1917 Skidmore had been indicted with seven others including Chicago Chief of Police Charles Healy for operating a graft connection between police and gamblers. Healy lost his job but neither he nor Skidmore did any jail time. When Anton Cermak took over the Cook County Board, Skidmore entered the junk business and received a lucrative county contract to handle scrap iron. He opened a junkyard at 2840 South Kedzie which became Skidmore's new headquarters. Skidmore worked for Jake "Greasy Thumb" Guzak as a contact man with city hall, the Kelly-Nash machine, and later to the state legislature. He aligned himself with Jake Zuta but still it was understood that Skidmore worked best for himself and made no pre-

---

4. Robey Street is no more, its name has been changed. Touhy's house still stands in its original place, Paddy the Bear's saloon is now a garage. Skidmore's saloon is a residence.

tenses that he could be trusted. In the early 1930s, he created a shakedown business where he approached the black policy kings like the Jones Brothers and assured them that for the paltry sum of $250 a week, the syndicate would not interfere in their operations. He would then go to the mob and offer them only half of the money he collected, keeping the rest for himself. By 1938, Skidmore had hundreds of deals in place with pimps, prostitutes, rogue cops and burglars.

Skidmore ran his operation out of his junkyard, the Lawndale Scrap Iron and Metal Company. It was there that Skidmore dispensed the mob's graft to police and politicians and collected protection from pimps and loan sharks who worked the rackets that the mob chose to avoid. Skidmore's other office, when he needed to speak to customers working out in the county, was the personal lair of Herbert Burns, the Chief of Cook County's Highway Patrol. Burns owed Skidmore a small fortune for gambling debts.

However, most of Billy's business was done at the junkyard, and it was here that newspaper reporters watched a Chicago police captain named Tom Harrison visit every Saturday morning for almost a year. Harrison said he went to buy fresh eggs for his family. Federal prosecutors said he owed Skidmore ten thousand dollars for gambling debts.

In 1939 the Cook County Chief of Police, Lester Laird, "declared war" on gambling. Needless to say, reporters from the *Chicago Tribune* were surprised to find the chief visiting Skidmore at his junkyard/handbook operation the day after his declaration of war. As it turns out, the chief had been calling on Skidmore four to six times a month over a five year period. He was also a frequent visitor to

Skidmore's 260-acre estate in McHenry, Illinois. When confronted by reporters about his visits to the Skidmore place, the chief replied that he had gone to personally harass Skidmore into obeying the law. That same afternoon, reporters followed Laird to the Drake Hotel where he had dinner with Skidmore. When a photographer snapped a picture of the two of them together, Laird leaped up from his table and ran out of the hotel through the kitchen.

He resigned the next day.

On March 20, 1942, Skidmore was found guilty of tax evasion and sentenced to Terre Haute prison for two-and-a-half years, plus $5,000 in penalties. Skidmore's cellmates were Sam Giancana and black policy king Edward Jones. Skidmore convinced Jones to acquaint Giancana with the numbers racket on the mostly black south side. When Giancana was released from prison, he and the remnants of the old 42 Gang, invaded the south side and took over the policy racket, eventually banishing Jones to Mexico.

As for Billy Skidmore, he never saw the light of another free day again. He died of cancer while still in prison in 1943.

Green met Henrichsen at Skidmore's junkyard. He knew that Henrichsen had landed the job with Skidmore through Tubbo Gilbert's influence. In fact, years later Henrichsen's widow swore out a statement that Gilbert had actually ordered Skidmore to give Henrichsen the job.

"He told me," Green recalled, "Tubbo Gilbert and Assistant States Attorney Crowley told me I had a choice of being a defendant or eating steaks at the States Attorney's expense. They said that if I ever got out of line they would indict me for kidnapping Factor and that I could get up there [on the stand] with Touhy and the others."

Green pushed for more information and Henrichsen eventually admitted that he and Eddie Schwabauer had been paid off by John Factor to lie on the witness stand. He said that he went to the Sycamore jail, where Factor was temporarily held after the kidnap trial ended pending a decision on his immigration status, and "I would meet him on the stairs there, me and Eddie Schwabauer, and Factor would pay us."

Green tried for the impossible. "Look, you know Touhy is innocent, I know Touhy's innocent on this thing, now why don't you do right by him and tell the truth about this to a judge?"

Henrichsen laughed it off. "Look, I got a wife and four kids and I got to provide for them, and I'm not going to do nothing that gets on the wrong side of Tubbo [Gilbert]...look, I got a choice here, I mean I could have testified the way I did and eat steaks at the County's expense or I could have been a defendant. They, Tubbo and Crowley and them, they told me real, real clear, they said I would be indicted right along with Roger and those fellows if I didn't testify the way they wanted."

Next, Green went to see Mrs. Sczech and her son, Eddie Schwabauer. It was Schwabauer who agreed to hide Factor in his mother's house on the night Factor kidnapped himself. Green pegged the pair the same way that Tubbo Gilbert did, as pushovers, so he took a gamble. He told them that he had absolute proof that Touhy was innocent and that it was only a matter of time before Buck Henrichsen swore out an affidavit stating that the mother and son had lied on the witness stand at the Factor kidnapping trials. It worked because they knew that Buck Henrichsen was a man who could not be trusted.

On advice from Touhy's lawyers, Green took Mrs. Sczech and Eddie Schwabauer to South Bend, Indiana to the office of a former U.S. Congressman where they confirmed a statement that laid out the kidnapping plan. They admitted lying on the witness stand, and their statement said that less than an hour after Factor's car was run off the road that Jake Factor appeared at Mrs. Sczech's home, not blindfolded or bound in any manner, and made several phone calls before retiring for the night.

When Mrs. Sczech and Schwabauer learned that Touhy's lawyers would have to file their statements as affidavits to the U.S. Supreme Court, they insisted on being moved to Canada for their own protection though Roger said, "few, if any, terrorists have the courage to harm or murder witnesses in United States Supreme Court cases."

Unfortunately, the Canadians turned the party around at the border, denying them entry. Instead Green hid them in a rented house in Kankakee until the papers were before the court.

Then Green went to Manard Prison and interviewed Touhy gang members Gus Schafer and Albert Kator, both of whom had been convicted with Touhy. "I was," Roger said, "a little hurt by what Morrie learned from them. They had in fact been in on the Factor hoax. Buck Henrichsen had brought them into the deal. They had shared in the $70,000 pay-off."

Years later in court, Schafer told Roger, "We were afraid to let you know. Anyway what in the by jesus good would it have done?"

Schafer and Kator told him that Buck Henrichsen had cut them in on the Factor kidnapping and had taken turns keeping Factor company at a house at Bangs Lake in Wauconda, Illinois.

Green found the house, and both its owner and the yardman gave sworn testimony that they had seen Factor around the property during the time that he was missing. They even went so far as to say that they had seen him taking walks around the lake alone on several occasions.

Next, Green found Harry Geils and Frankie Brown, the comedy team hired by Henrichsen to entertain Factor while he was in hiding. Each gave their statements that Factor wasn't tied up when they saw him. In fact, they had shared drinks together.

Green interviewed Chicago policemen Walter Miller and Lieutenant Thomas J. Maloney who had worked for Tubbo Gilbert and had been assigned to guard Factor after his reappearance in La Grange. Factor had told both of them that he never saw his kidnappers and had no idea what they looked like.

Green then traveled to Knoxville, Tennessee, and picked up sworn statements from a woman who testified that on the night Factor was kidnapped she had been out to the wrestling matches with Ike Costner and Basil Banghart at the Lyric Theater in Knoxville.

Green returned to Statesville and reported everything to Roger who doubled over with joy. Based on the evidence that Green had uncovered, Roger's lawyers prepared a brilliant appeal for the Illinois State Supreme Court. But their appeal was denied without a hearing, as was another appeal placed before the United States Supreme Court. Then, Robert Lally, a newspaper reporter with the once powerful Chicago *Daily News* who had taken up Roger's cause, died of cancer. Lally had worked closely with Morrie Green and had even developed his own information which he assured Roger would get him out of jail.

"His death," Roger said, "saddened and shocked me, partly for selfish reasons, I'll admit...Lally kept telling me that he had proof to get me out, that I would never spend another Christmas in Stateville. I believed him and I still think he had something big, although I never learned what it was...I was now as dead, legally speaking, as the old broken-down cons who get a $27 funeral at the state's expense, in a prison made burial suit, out of Stateville. The difference was that I hadn't been embalmed."

It was at that point Roger decided to escape from Stateville.

Escape From the Big House

Roger never accepted his conviction for kidnapping John Factor.

After seven years in prison, he became a jailhouse lawyer, pouring over his court transcripts, and as a result became something of an expert in the writ of *habeas corpus*.[5] He wrote his own appeals to the governor but after a while they were returned unopened.

Of his frustration Touhy wrote,

> Denied without a hearing...denied without a hearing...denied without a hearing....How could I get justice if no court would listen to me? I was nailed in a box and I had no hammer to batter my way out.

Then, in the latter part of August, 1942, Touhy decided to escape from prison for a somewhat peculiar reason.

> I stayed awake until dawn in my cell, thinking. I was without hope. I was buried alive in prison and

---

5. Not all of his time was spent in the prison law library. Prison officials suspected Touhy was the boss of Stateville's enormous Irish gang which ruled over the facility's black market. Gambling belonged to the Italian gangs. In fact, on Touhy's first month in prison he was disciplined for sanctioning and supervising the beating of another prisoner.

I would die there. I couldn't see a light ahead anywhere. Nothing but darkness and loneliness and
desperation. The world had forgotten me after eight
years. I was a nothing. Well, there was one way I
could focus public attention on my misery. I could
escape. I would be caught of course but the break
would show my terrible situation. What cockeyed
thinking that was....my mental attitude was a
mess, I later came to realize.

The inmate who came to him with the idea of
escaping was Gene O'Connor, who had probably
known Roger on the outside, since O'Connor had
been the business agent of the Chicago Awning and
Tent Makers Union—or at least he was until he was
arrested for intimidation after firing a shot at a
union member who opposed him in a race.

Now, O'Connor was serving a life sentence for a
May 1932 robbery in which a Chicago policeman
had been gunned down in cold blood.

Escaping for O'Connor was a way of life. In 1936
he escaped from Statesville after he found his way
into the central electric room, pulled the main power
switch and then scaled the walls to freedom. He was
captured and escaped again a year later only to be
caught within a week.

The time seemed ripe again for escape. The war
had taken away the younger guards, leaving mostly
older men, some coming out of retirement to resume
duty. Since they were paid starvation wages,
O'Connor had primed the escape by bribing the
tower guards with items lifted from prison kitchen
storehouses where Touhy worked. These foods were
almost impossible to get during wartime rationing:
100 pound sacks of sugar, bags of coffee, slabs of
bacon and quarter sides of beef all of which could be
resold on the outside for big money. Adding to the

plan's credibility was the fact that E.H. Stubenfield, an old time political hack, was now warden. He had replaced the far better qualified Joseph Ragen, who had resigned in protest against political meddling inside the prison. As a result, the prison's once tight security had gone lax.

The keys to the escape were guns. Two pistols were left at the base of the prison's flagpole by the brother of another inmate, Eddie Darlak, who was in on the break. A trustee had brought two guns into the prison, carried inside wrapped in the American flag which he lowered each evening outside the prison walls.

On October 9, 1942, Roger stood at the prison bakery door with an enormous pair of scissors stolen from the tailor shop, hidden inside of his blue prison-issue shirt. Several minutes later, driver Jack Cito, a convict with mob connections,[6] pulled the prison laundry truck up to the door and Roger leaped up onto the driver's door and yanked Cito out on to the ground and screamed for the keys. When Cito moved too slowly, Touhy cut him with the scissors, yelling "Give me the Goddamn keys!"

Cito told Touhy the keys were in the ignition and Roger leaped into the truck and drove to the mechanic shop where the other escapees, O'Connor, McInerney, Darlak, Stewart and Nelson were waiting.

Touhy leaped out of the truck and O'Connor handed him a .45 caliber automatic. He rushed into the mechanic shop where he was confronted by a guard, Lieutenant Samuel Johnston, who asked

---

6. Jack Cito's first arrest came in distinguished company. Cito and legendary labor goon Maxie Eisen, on May 29, 1927, were arrested for carrying concealed weapons. Actually the two pistols were later found in a secret compartment of Cito's car. But, since they didn't have the guns on their persons the judge dropped the charges. Cito's brother was an enforcer in the Capone organization.

Touhy "Why are you here, what are you doing here?"

Roger didn't answer but began snapping the prison telephone wires with his long scissors. As Johnston was about to club Touhy into submission, Basil Banghart came through the window with a pistol at ready and ordered Johnston to unlock a set of ladders. At that same moment, guard George Cotter arrived on the scene and was overpowered and beaten to the floor.

Placing the guards' white hats on their heads, they pushed Cotter and Johnston outside and forced them to load the ladders on to the back of the truck and ordered them to sit on the ladders to keep them from falling off. Then Roger shouted, "Ok, go, go go!" at Stewart, who was behind the wheel, but the truck stalled.

Touhy leaped off the back of the vehicle, pulled Stewart out of the driver's seat and tried to get the truck started but couldn't. Deciding to jump start the truck, Roger looked over to the 300 inmates crowding around to watch the excitement. Roger yelled for the convicts to push the truck, which they did. The motor turned over with a roar.

They sped across the yard, driving to Tower Three in the northwest corner. At the base of the tower they forced guard Johnston to help them put the ladders together. When he refused, they beat him, tore his shirt off and took him up the ladder with them. Roger looked up into the tower and could see one of the guards who they had bribed[7] standing to one side of the tower, at the end of the walkway. "He wasn't holding a gun but he didn't have far to reach for one," Touhy said.

Roger fired a single shot which blew out the

7. After the escape, the Illinois Governor conducted his own investigation and personally fired the guard, sixty-two-year old-Herman Krause.

guardhouse window, striking the guard in the forehead with flying glass and knocking him to the floor. When they were all inside the tower, Darlak[8] took the guard's car keys. Though it was against prison regulations, the car was parked at the base of the prison wall, just feet away from the tower.

Before leaving, the convicts took two high-powered prison-issue rifles, a pistol and 115 to 120 rounds for each gun. They then walked calmly down the tower stairs, into Krause's car, and roared away toward Chicago.

During the first three days after the escape, there were reports of them being spotted in all of the Chicago suburbs and most of the United States. However, by the second week news from the war in Europe had pushed them off of the front pages and they were, for the most part, forgotten about.

Through Roger's contacts on the outside they were able to rent a large apartment in a run down tenement building not far from the Valley, where Roger had grown up. There, the escaped convicts lived quietly for two months. By early December, they began to quarrel, largely because Nelson and McInerney had begun drinking and talking about going out for women. Roger told them to stop drinking and to forget about women for at least another three months. Nelson didn't like it; he threw a punch that started a brawl. The brawl brought the neighbors banging on the door. The next morning Roger moved out into his own place.

For the first few days, Roger sat around his small apartment "admiring the loneliness." His solitude didn't last long though, he eventually made contact with his brother, Eddie, who provided him

---

8. Darlak was also armed with a homemade gasoline bomb that was to be used only in the event that they were cornered in a shootout.

with a bankroll of $2,500 and a plan to send him to Arizona.

Using the money Eddie had given him but refusing to leave Chicago, Roger took $200 of the money and was able to get a driver's license, Social Security card and a military draft card (an absolute must in 1942). With these papers Touhy took on the identity of Robert Jackson who was exempt from military service because he worked in a war plant. Touhy even had a small metal badge that read "Inspector" which he wore on his lapel.

"I wore good clothes," Roger said, "but nothing gaudy. My hat came down well on my forehead. I wore glasses issued to me in prison and the old photographs of me in the paper showed me without them...."

He bought a used car and spent his days driving through the forest preserves or going to the movies.

Six weeks went by before he saw Basil Banghart, the only escapee who knew where Roger lived. Banghart began to visit regularly and on one visit he asked Roger to come over to the apartment. Since Roger was lonely and bored, he took him up on the offer on Thanksgiving and stayed the night. The next day all seven were playing cards and drinking when another fist fight broke out.

Touhy remembers,

> The time was getting close for capture. The Christmas season came along and I spent hours walking State Street looking in the windows...lonely as a whorehouse on Christmas eve...well I lived it...in a side street saloon, listening to the Christmas carols on the radio and drinking beer for beer with a white haired bartender...the next day I went to the Empire Room in the Palmer House, got a table in a corner and

ate a big dinner...freedom was beginning to pall on me, I guess.

Roger's landlady had left him a Christmas gift in his room, so he stopped by her apartment to thank her. While he was there, one of her guests spotted him and Roger, with a convict's sixth sense, knew he had been made. That night he moved back in with Banghart and the others.

The transition back to living with the others didn't go well. There was another fist fight and Nelson and Stewart left the apartment shortly after Touhy's return. Nelson went to Minneapolis where his mother turned him in to the FBI just hours after he arrived. Within minutes after his arrest, Nelson told the agents everything he knew about the escapees and by nightfall, a small army of agents was slowly and carefully moving in around the gang's apartments.

J. Edgar Hoover arrived on the scene to personally supervise the raid because he felt that Touhy had sullied the Bureau's reputation when he escaped conviction from the Hamm kidnapping case built by Special Agent Purvis back in 1933. To Hoover, the FBI's capture of Touhy would justify the Bureau's original campaign to put him behind bars. Legally, Touhy and the others hadn't done anything wrong. Incredibly there was no law in the state of Illinois against escaping from prison nor would there be one until 1949. Even if there were such a law, as a federal agency, the FBI still had no grounds to enter the case. Hoover needed a reason to lock Touhy up so his brain trust created one. It was decided that Touhy and the others had violated the federal law which required all men of military age to notify their draft boards when they had changed addresses. The fact that Roger was well over draft age and had already served his country and that the others as convicted felons weren't required to register were only facts that clogged the theory.

The FBI's Chicago office had the entire arrest procedure planned out days in advance of Hoover's arrival. Agents and snipers already surrounded the building and undercover agents had rented several apartments in the building.

When O'Connor and McInerney came home, six agents, guns drawn, leaped out from behind a hall-way door.

"Put your hands up! We're federal officers!"

O'Connor turned, and according to agents' reports, fired his .45 caliber automatic twice, with the bullets ending up in the stair rail. McInerney never got to reach for his .38 caliber; the agents returned fire and pumped at least thirty-five shells into the two convicts.

Roger and Banghart arrived back at the apart-ment about an hour later. Recalling the incident Touhy wrote, "We went to the Kenmore flat and up the back stairway after I had parked the car a block away...the joint felt creepy to me, and I prowled around uneasy as an alley tomcat at midnight mat-ing time and peered out the windows."

At zero hour, powerful search lights were turned on to the windows of Touhy's apartment and then a loud speaker cracked the silence of the night with "Roger Touhy and the other escaped convicts! The building is surrounded. We are about to throw tear gas in the building. Surrender now and you will not be killed."

Banghart wanted to shoot it out, but Roger negated this move. They debated over what to do for the next ten minutes before Banghart shouted out the window "We're coming out!"

"Then come out backward with your hands high in the air! Banghart, you come out first."

Banghart, wearing only his pants, appeared at the front door, his back to the agents. Roger, clad in fire-engine-red pajamas, followed him.

The agents leaped on each of them as they came out of the building and knocked them to the freezing cold pavement and handcuffed them.

A dozen agents rushed into the apartment and found five pistols, three sawed off shotguns, a .30.30 rifle and $13,523 in cash which they handed over to Tubbo Gilbert who was still the Chief Investigator for the States Attorney's Office.

When Gilbert returned the cash to the prisoners at Stateville prison, he said that he had only been given $800 by the FBI.

After Touhy and Banghart were handcuffed, J. Edgar Hoover, surrounded by a dozen agents and a dozen more newspaper reporters, strolled up to Banghart and said "Well, Banghart, you're a trapped rat."

Banghart burst out into a huge smile. "You're J. Edgar Hoover aren't you?" he asked.

"Yes," Hoover beamed, "I am."

Banghart nodded his head and said, "You're a lot fatter in person than you are on the radio."

Later the next day, Warden Joseph Ragen came to the Cook County criminal courts building to collect his prisoners. When Touhy, who had chains around his waist, ankles and wrists saw him he said, "Well Warden, looks like I got you your old job back."

Ragen nodded and smiled at the irony "Yes, Touhy, it looks like you did."

A parade of eight cars filled with four heavily armed States Attorney's detectives drove the prisoners back to Stateville. Each was sent to solitary confinement where they survived on bread and water with a full meal every third day.

Roger was taken out of solitary several days later and brought before a judge who told him, to his amazement, that his sentence was now 199 years because under a little known Illinois law, anyone who abets the escape of a state prisoner receives the same sentence as the prisoner they helped escape. The state of Illinois had decided that Touhy should take on Eddie Darlak's sentence of 100 years.

Roger was the first person to be given this sentence under that law. State authorities had had enough of Banghart and his death-defying escapes. He was becoming a convict legend. A week after he was returned to Stateville, Banghart was hauled out of solitary confinement and shipped off to the island prison at Alcatraz. It was a stroke of bad luck for Banghart, because although he could fly a plane and drive a car better and faster than most mere mortals, he had never learned to swim.

Several months after Touhy's return to prison, 20th-Century Fox began production of *Roger Touhy, Last of the Gangsters* which was released in 1948 as *Roger Touhy—Gangster.*

The syndicate couldn't get the movie done quickly enough. Touhy's escape was a godsend. He had dug his own hole and through their enormous influence in the film industry, they were going to provide the celluloid coffin for him.

The film's producer would be Bryan Foy, and like some people associated with the film industry then, he was a man with a past. From a creative standpoint, he was a logical choice because he specialized in gritty realistic film noir, but he wasn't, as he so often said, "married to the higher concept of film as art." Foy would and did shoot whatever would turn a dollar from *PT 109* to *Women's Prison*.

Foy's actual standing was somewhere in between important films and "B" films. In fact, by 1935 Foy had produced so many "B" films that he was known as the king of "B" pictures. He often joked that he made the same film 100 times using different locations and different actors. Still, almost every one of Foy's low-budget movies were box-office money makers.

Foy is still considered one of the most prolific film producers in Hollywood's history. He had helped to bring the industry into the sound age while he was at Warner Brothers, then nothing more then a collection of buildings and second-hand film equipment. Foy produced the first all talkie for Warners in 1928, *Lights of New York* and became popular for turning out program films.

A Chicagoan, Bryan Foy was the eldest son of vaudeville comedian Eddie Foy whose seven children became the traveling stage act "The Seven Little Foys." Bryan moved to Los Angeles in 1922 and grew up with the film industry, eventually becoming a film producer, sometimes producing as many as thirty films a year

Like anyone else who grew up in show business at the time, Foy learned early on that it was to his best advantage to rub shoulders with the hoods who dominated the industry and night clubs across the country. As a result, Foy's Beverly Hills houseguests would often include Chicago's political boss Ed Kelly or Allen Smiley, a shadowy L.A. figure whose fingers were in a dozen different pies. As an FBI informant working inside Hollywood reported to Washington, "Foy has a reputation within the industry for hiring ex-convicts or hoodlums who come out to Hollywood in search of work."

"Brynie," said a friend, "was always close to people who lived on the edge of right and wrong."

Interestingly, John Factor and Foy had been friends for years and Factor had once been a houseguest at Foy's estate. There he met a young actor named Ronald Reagan, whose films Foy produced at Warners. Over the years, Foy's younger brother Eddie Jr. was featured in three of Reagan's movies. "I soon learned," Reagan wrote, "that I could go in to Brynie and tell him that I had been laid off, but couldn't take it at the moment because of all my expenses. He would pick up the phone, call a couple of henchmen and actually get the picture going on four or five days notice—just to put me back on salary."

Foy left Warner Brothers after a dispute with Jack Warner. After his stint with Warner he was named president of Eagle-Lion Studios, a British-based film production company. One of Foy's first acts as boss was to hire Johnny Rosselli—Chicago's west coast contact—as a producer. This happened as Rosselli was released from Atlanta federal prison where he had served only two years of a six-year sentence.

Foy liked Rosselli. They were both tough talking, street smart and savvy. Foy thought Rosselli was a handsome man, always dapper, who appreciated fine restaurants and chic Hollywood parties and like Foy was a devoted and knowledgeable fan of the film business. Sure, Rosselli was a tough gangster. Foy knew that of course, but it was a side of his friend that he had never seen displayed.

Foy remained close to Rosselli throughout most of the late 1940s and early 1950s. Rosselli spent weekends at Foy's house and whenever he could,

Foy put him on the books in one no-show position after another. "They were like the Rover boys," Foy's niece said. "They went everywhere together."

Despite Foy's financial success at Eagle-Lion studios, his brash confrontational style irritated the studio brass so when Foy's three-year contract expired in 1950 he was released. He bounced back to Warner Brothers but couldn't take Rosselli with him since the studio had barred him from the lot. But Foy and Rosselli stayed in close contact. In fact, Foy introduced Rosselli to one of his favorite contract players at Warner, Bill Campbell, who lived in the same neighborhood as Rosselli. In turn Bill Campbell introduced Rosselli to his young wife, actress Judy Campbell, who would later have affairs with Rosselli's boss, Sam Giancana, Frank Sinatra and President John F. Kennedy among many others.

When Foy's wife Vivian was suffering with cancer in 1949, Rosselli all but moved into the house. Foy's daughter, Madeline Foy O'Donnell recalled that, "Brynie happened to be out of the house for a while, and I guess the kids were somewhere else in the house, but Johnny was sitting with Vivian when she died. He closed her eyes."

Eventually Foy and Rosselli had a falling out when in 1954, Foy crossed one of Rosselli's brothers in a business deal. Rosselli confronted Foy but he refused to back down causing Rosselli to slug the producer, knocking him to the ground. It would be ten years before the two men would talk to each other again.

There was another mob connection to the film as well.

One of the law firms representing 20th-Century Fox was owned by Sidney Korshak, an alleged associate of the underworld. Korshak's brother was a partner with Tony Accardo in a casino run out of a storefront on Rush Street in Chicago. It was one of the most profitable casinos in the country. Korshak's firm had also represented George Browne, Willie Bioff, Paul Ricca, Tony Accardo and a slew of other Chicago- and L.A.- based hoods over the years.

The film script about Touhy's escape was written in less than thirty days. It was written while Touhy was still at large, so the writers centered the plot of the film on the escape and not its aftermath. Foy said that the script was still being written when Touhy was recaptured. Fox purchased the concept and ordered it rewritten by Crane Wilbur and Jerry Cady, both veteran Hollywood writers and directors.

Afterward, Fox sent the executive producer, Lee Marcus, and the director, Robert Florey to Chicago in January of 1943 just a few days after the capture to photograph actual locations for the scenes.

Years later, when questioned about the rush to get the film made, Fox executives associated with the film said they wanted to capitalize on the headlines. Fox wanted the picture rushed through production before the public forgot about Touhy.

Robert Florey recalls,

> The shooting at 1254-56 Leland Avenue had taken place just a few days before and the place was a mess. For a week at Joliet the warden allowed us to shoot many scenes and places inside and in the courtyard using trustees as doubles and producing the escape scene in long shots. The Mayor and the Chief of Police helped him in every way and he was allowed to interview Touhy and the others. The film was completed in a remarkable thirty-three days back on the sound stages.

For the most part, the script refrained from using any real names except for the syndicate's enemies, Roger Touhy and Basil Banghart, and yet Fox was threatened by a lawsuit from Jake the Barber.

Then, to Hollywood's surprise, Roger Touhy sued Fox Studios and its distributors on the grounds that the film defamed him. Suit or no suit, the film previewed at Stateville prison on July 12, 1943. Over one thousand state officials watched in the prison's main yard.

Jacob Arvey, Cook County Chairman and a "close personal friend" of Jake the Barber and Tubbo Gilbert, had a front row seat. Roger Touhy, who refused to attend, sat in his darkened cell where he could hear the echo from the film's dialogue which he believed ridiculed him.

No one had ever seen anything like this film before. It was the pioneer of the quasi-documentary technique that two years later would become the trademark of semi-factual exposes. The *mise-en-scène* of the film was groundbreaking. The escape scene was shot entirely in long-shot. This technique made the film look more like a newsreel than the feature films that people were used to. Finally, the film concludes with an on-camera speech by Statesville Warden Joseph Ragan.

Illinois state officials loved every second of the film. On the other hand, when the FBI saw it, they hated it. In fact, J. Edgar Hoover objected to the film before he saw it. Upon seeing it, Hoover objected to several scenes in which local police were given credit for FBI work. He was also generally displeased with being mentioned in the film at all. Hoover wanted the public to forget Touhy. The Hamm trial was still an ugly stench. In fact, when Hoover allowed the official story of the FBI—*The FBI Story* and later *The FBI Nobody Knows*—to be written, there was no mention of the Hamm case or Roger Touhy. Despite the fact that the FBI took credit for the capture, the agency demanded that a disclaimer be included to alert the public that the portrayal of agents in a movie did not constitute an endorsement of the film and should not be construed as a seal of approval. At that point, Fox considered shelving the picture. More than a year later they finally released it. By that time the escape was all but forgotten. Even after waiting a year to release the film, the studio did so with caution. The producer's press book came complete with a statement that read, "We wouldn't be justified in making a picture about Touhy except that he is representative of the era and happily, a passing of it."

Foy said that his inspiration for the film was not the sudden flush of money that came out of cash-strapped Fox, but rather that "it was the dragnet for him [Touhy]; it was the most expensive in the history of the city and when the FBI made it a nation-wide manhunt it became the most expansive man-hunt in history for an escaped prisoner, and with nothing but bad news coming from the war front in those days it [the escape] was like a return to the old days of a decade before."

The Hays Office (Hollywood's self-censorship organization) demanded and received a cut in the film. They wanted one entire reel cut on the grounds of extreme violence. They felt it was "bad for the general public," said Florey.

Preston Foster, fresh off of a string of profitable films, portrayed Roger Touhy not as a hero or a vil-lain, but as a cardboard character who lacked any appeal in any manner. Preston's version of Touhy is as a petty, mean, calculating little man. The film portrayed him as a "two-bit ugly little punk robbed of any sympathy," as one reviewer put it.

When the film flopped at theaters under the title *Roger Touhy—Gangster!*, it was renamed *Roger Touhy, Last of the Gangsters*, which was actually the first title Foy had given to the film before production started. But the film failed at the box office for more than just its title. It failed for the same reason Touhy's escape from Statesville failed: it failed to rally the people to his cause.

The film attempted to define Roger Touhy as an astrology buff who began the day of his prison break by reading a Scorpio horoscope, "A new door opens for you, the future is assured."

"I won't let them forget me," he says, assuring one and all of his Napoleonic complex.

On August 4, 1943, Roger Touhy managed to get a temporary restriction on showing the film which, he argued, portrayed him "as a vicious violator and gangster." But on August 7, 1943 Fox Studios managed to have the ban lifted. Oddly enough Touhy never made a public mention of the film or his troubles with Hollywood nor did he note it in his autobiography *The Stolen Years*.

In 1948, Touhy won an out of court settlement with Fox and its distributors. Touhy accepted a settlement of $10,000 for defamation of character and an agreement by Fox to destroy the film. Within a week, Touhy's lawyers had his $10,000 and Fox started to redistribute the film overseas.

• • •

Domestic security and patriotism were front and center in wartime Chicago and in the nation. All efforts by the citizenry were devoted to success in defeating the enemy. As a result, the gangster figure all but vanished from the silver screen between

1941 and 1946. It was replaced by spy and war stories featuring Nazi or Japanese villains. The failure of the film reflected a larger cultural shift that left the old-time gangster as a relic for the history books.

The Lawyer

After his return to prison, Roger's faith that he would ever see freedom again was badly shaken. However, in 1948 his lawyer, Howard Bryant, brought another attorney named Robert B. Johnstone into the case. Johnstone was a tough, forty-three-year-old, seldom-smiling, giant of a man who rarely spoke unless spoken to.

"You had the impression," Betty Brennan said "that he was angry all the time...frankly he scared me a little bit. I mean he was such an imposing man, so different from Mr. Touhy in every way. Later, I learned that he was basically a shy, desperately uncomfortable, gentle man."

Roger wrote "Johnstone [was] a determined—sometimes obstinate and irascible—man...strong-willed about many things, both important and trivial. I watched him as he strode the length of the long, narrow room and climbed a short flight of steps at the end. He was a big man and he leaned forward a little when he walked. His mop of black hair could have used some grooming and his blue suit looked as if it might have been fitted to him by a tailor with astigmatism. I had confidence in the guy. I knew somehow he would do his damnest for me."

Upon reviewing the case, what caught Johnstone's attention was the report prepared by Morrie Green, the private detective Touhy hired after his conviction. Now, more than four years after his investigation ended, Touhy and Johnstone sat in the attorney's visiting room at Statesville going over Morrie Green's report.

With Green's research in hand, Johnstone set out to free Touhy legally. He began by cross-examining Touhy like the criminal trial lawyer he was. He tried to trap him in a lie or a contradiction, but he couldn't. "Johnstone was no starry-eyed dreamer. At the end he gazed at me in silence for two or three minutes and then burst forth with the hoarse voice he used at times of stress or strong emotion. "I'm a damn fool Touhy, but I'll take the case if you want me to."

There were some last minute warnings by Johnstone not to expect any miracles and then he grabbed his briefcase and left. "I was back in my cell before I realized that he hadn't mentioned a fee. I would pay him what I could, of course, but it was heartening to know that his first concern wasn't money."

Robert Johnstone wasn't one to show his emotion and he wasn't about to display them to Roger Touhy, but when he returned to his office, he turned his case load over to other attorneys and told his secretary that his focus would be on Touhy. "Within a few minutes he kicked away a law practice that had taken him years to build....He didn't give a damn...he not only wrecked his career but he also messed up his health working for me. What can I say about him? Only that he is the best friend a convict ever had."

It wasn't all mutual admiration of course, because Roger could be just as obstinate as Bob Johnstone. Worse yet, fourteen years in the Statesville prison library had turned Touhy into a fairly competent jail-house lawyer who was used to overriding and outshouting his legal counsel. As a result he and Johnstone argued strategy often and loudly. "Johnstone [was] a determined man," Roger said, "sometimes obstinate and irascible, strong willed about many things, both important and trivial." After four months of working together in close quarters in April of 1948, Johnstone told Roger, in his usual brisk fashion, that it was time to bring Clara and the boys up from Florida. "They should be with you at this time. I'll make arrangements through your sisters."

It had been years since Roger had last seen his wife and sons. Roger wrote:

> ...I couldn't forget her last visit. It had been an ordeal rather than the usual delight. She had worn a white hat and gloves and a dark tailored suit, I remember...at that time, in 1938, I had been disconsolate. I had figured that I couldn't be a drag on Clara and our two sons for all of their lives. So I had given her a direct order for the first time in our marriage; take all the money you can raise and go to Florida. Change your name. Take the kids with you, of course. Start them out in a new school down there under new names. This is something you must do.

After that, Clara and the boys left for Delano, Florida where they would live under the name of Turner.

Now, ten years later, as badly as Roger wanted to see Clara and the boys he refused to see her. "I told him," Touhy said, "he wouldn't do any such damn thing. Clara had managed to set up a life for herself and the boys. Roger Jr. and Tommy were of college age. I wasn't going to do anything to screw up their future."

Johnstone knew that Roger had misunderstood the situation outside of Statesville. Clara and their sons had contacted Johnstone, not the other way around. The boys, now in their twenties, wanted to see their father and Clara desired to see her husband...convict or no convict. "They want to show you," Johnstone told Touhy "that they have faith in you. They have that right."

Roger refused to give in, but Johnstone set up the reunion anyway. On April 22, 1948, Roger and Clara's twenty-sixth wedding anniversary, Clara and the boys came to Statesville.

My heart did a flip flop. My knees turned rubbery. There they were—Clara and our two fine sons. They were looking up at me smiling...I sat opposite to them, and I realized that I was wearing a silly grin. I was never happier...it was ten years since I saw Clara. There were lines in her face and gray in her hair, but she was pretty...I thought our sons were handsome. That's a father's privilege.

They talked non-stop for an hour. Roger asked his sons in a man-to-man fashion how it felt to visit their father in prison and then braced himself for the worst. The boys said that their mother had explained the situation as soon as they were old enough to understand. "[They] were never ashamed," Touhy wrote. "I felt grand as I walked through the yard back to my cell. I was a family man again. I would ask for a spade or a trowel the next day, by God, and go out and plant some flowers...."

A few days later, Roger sat across from Johnstone and tried to thank him for setting up the visit, to try and tell him that he was right to bring Clara and the boys back to Chicago, but Johnstone, not one for public displays of emotion, brushed it aside and got down to business. Johnstone said that the key to unlocking the case was to bring Isaac Costner over to Roger's side. He felt that after fourteen years in prison there was a chance that Costner might cooperate.

Johnstone flew to Leavenworth Prison and with little prompting, Costner told him everything he wanted to hear. Costner even signed an affidavit that he had been persuaded to perjure himself at the second Factor kidnapping trial in 1934, by Jake the Barber and Tubbo Gilbert—in effect the prosecution. Armed with Costner's testimony and combined with the outstanding leg work done by Morrie Green, Johnstone filed for a hearing before the federal court's most unpredictable judge, John P. Barnes, "the bearded dean of the federal bench in the Northern District of Illinois."

The Appeal

At age seventy-three, John Barnes had a reputation as a stern but fair jurist. He was tall, waspy, bearded and withdrawn, with a deep imposing voice to match. It seemed like Barnes had been sent to the bench by Hollywood's Central Casting. Barnes was appointed to the Federal bench on February 27, 1931 and gained national attention in March of 1936 when he held that Roosevelt's National Recovery Act (NRA) was unconstitutional. He was eventually overruled by the United States Supreme Court, but the move earned the judge a reputation in Washington and Chicago as an odd-ball who wouldn't go along with the program.

Odd-ball or not, the Chicago Crime Commission called Barnes the most reliably honest judge in the state. That was a powerful statement. Barnes' actual personality was a far cry from his kindly old grandfather image. Robert Johnstone's request for the FBI's records on Roger Touhy was rejected by the FBI; a subpoena was issued to the FBI's special agent in charge of the Chicago office, Robert McSwain. Called to the witness stand on June 2,

1949, Barnes asked Agent McSwain, "Have you produced the documents in response to the subpoena given you?"

"No, sir, I have not."

"Will you produce them?"

"I must respectfully advise the court that under instruction to me by the Attorney General...."

Barnes interrupted, "Then I hold you in contempt of court, and order you be held in my jail until you or your superiors have reconsidered this stance. The bailiff will disarm and escort Special Agent McSwain from the court room."

McSwain was released two days later when the Chief Judge held that an employee of the federal government could not be held liable for following orders of that government in relation to its refusal to release documents and data it considered sensitive. It turned out that the only thing that the FBI documents would have revealed was that back in 1933, Special Agent Melvin Purvis had been aware that the States Attorney's office had Roger Touhy's lawyer's phone bugged during both Factor kidnap trials: information that he never revealed to the presiding judge, which as an attorney he was obligated to so do.

When the hearings started, Johnstone fired off the first volley by getting a subpoena for all of the States Attorney's office records on the Factor case, but to his disappointment, the records didn't include a statement that Factor had given in which he said he could not identify any of his kidnappers. Also missing from the files were copies of the transcripts of Touhy's lawyer's conversations that were illegally recorded by Tubbo Gilbert during the Hamm and Factor kidnapping trials.

Johnstone called fifty-seven witnesses, including

private detective Morrie Green, and Walter Miller and John Maloney—the two Chicago policemen assigned to protect Factor during the two kidnapping trials. Gus Schafer [9] was summoned, Albert Kator's [10] testimony was read. Basil Banghart gave his version of the events as did Isaac Costner.

Buck Henrichsen, Factor's probable kidnapper, couldn't be called to testify. He had died in 1943 while Touhy was on the loose from Stateville prison. A heart attack killed him just two hours before Touhy and Banghart, the men he had sent to jail, were recaptured by the FBI. He was forty-three years old. His family blamed the stress of Touhy's escape and the lack of protection offered to him by the Cook County States Attorney's office for his death.

Robert Johnstone was an intense man and the case was all consuming for him. Soon his health and mental state had deteriorated to the point where it concerned Touhy. "He was as tense as a spring that had been coiled to the breaking point. He was edgy, so full of the Touhy case and so outraged by the injustice that he seemed ready to explode at any time. I tried to warn him to relax a little. The only result was that he lost his temper."

One day, during a break in the hearing, Johnstone collapsed in the hall and had to be hospitalized for a nervous condition. His condition delayed Roger's case by eight months. The initial delay was followed by almost two years of legal maneuvering by the state. Finally, in the spring of 1954, Barnes heard the last testimony in the case and drew it to a close.

9. Schafer was still incarcerated at Stateville at the time, where he was a model prisoner and trustee.
10. Kator had died in Stateville under questionable circumstances in 1938.

On August 9, 1954, a cool summer day, Judge Barnes ordered Roger brought before the court to hear a summary of his decision. The decision was 1,556 pages long and included 216 pages of notes. Roger's wife Clara sat with a press corps that had suddenly decided to take up Roger's cause to hear the summary. She watched Roger being escorted into the courtroom in leg irons and handcuffs and heard Johnstone remark "You know Rog, I don't think you'll be wearing those things again."

Barnes entered the courtroom and seated himself behind the elevated bench and stared out over the room. "In his own dignified way," Roger noted, "he had a fine sense of timing and dramatics."

Finally, Barnes spoke. Roger remembered later that he was listening so intently to the judge's every word that he had blocked out the sounds of the traffic on the street below. He started his summary by reading that he had reached the conclusions that Roger Touhy had not kidnapped John Factor but rather that "John Factor was not kidnapped for ransom or otherwise on the nights of June 30-July 1, 1933, but was taken as a result of his own convenience, that John Factor's disappearance was a hoax meant only to forestall his extradition to Europe to avoid prosecution there."

Furthermore, Barnes ruled that Roger's conviction was procured on perjured testimony with the full knowledge of Captain Daniel Gilbert and States Attorney Courtney. He did spare Crowley, saying that he believed he had presented the evidence without knowing it was perjured.

Barnes also found that Gilbert's power in the office far exceeded that of any other law enforcement official before or since. He also found that Gilbert's boss Thomas Courtney was to be held responsible for Gilbert's actions.

"To put it mildly, Touhy was not an acceptable person to Captain Gilbert," Barnes read, "Touhy and the opposition with which he was identified were obstacles in the drive of the politico-criminal Capone syndicate to control and dominate the labor unions during the period right after the Factor affair. The criminal syndicate could not operate without the approval of the prosecutor's office which at that time was controlled by Courtney and Gilbert. They did continue to operate and to thrive without interference from Courtney and Gilbert. That the arrangement between Gilbert and the syndicate was closer than a mere tolerance, is evident from his function as a go-between for Horan and Wallace surrenders and from the fact that his men were put in key positions in the Capone dominated unions."

He went on to say that "the Department of Justice showed an astounding disregard for Touhy's rights and indulged in practices which cannot be condoned."

Barnes further ruled that Touhy "was deprived of the effective assistance of council devoted exclusively to the protection of his interest and was compelled against his will to accept the services of a counsel who was compelled to serve adverse interests."

Barnes also said that the Illinois statute under which Roger was sentenced to an additional 100 years for aiding Eddie Darlak's escape back in 1942 was unconstitutional and that Touhy's sentence under that statute was void as a result. He ended the hearing by pointing out that Touhy had never been connected to a capital crime, nor was he listed with the Chicago Crime Commission. From there Barnes went on to broadside the FBI, the Chicago Police, the Cook County States Attorney's Office and the syndicate.

Stroking his beard, Barnes finished reading his decision in slow, flat midwestern tones, "This court finds that John Factor was not kidnapped for ransom, or otherwise, on the night of June 30 or July 1st 1933, though he was taken as a result of his own connivance....This court further finds that Roger Touhy did not kidnap John Factor and in fact had no part in the alleged kidnapping of John Factor."

When Roger heard Barnes read the words "the relator, Roger Touhy, should forthwith be discharged from custody" he stood bolt upright, trembling and wept.

An army of reporters dashed from the courtroom to the line of wooden phone booths that lined the lobby wall while dozens of people circled Roger to congratulate him as Johnstone tried to pull him from his seat.

Roger walked from the courtroom a free man. Bailiffs, sheriffs' deputies, courtroom employees and passersby crowded around him and shook his hand and slapped his back as he, Clara and Johnstone walked downstairs to the coffee shop. A few secretaries came out and asked for his autograph but he politely declined. "Oh please, not that, thank you, darling." In the coffee shop he remembered dropping a sugar bowl. He wrote, "The bowl broke and sugar cubes went all over the table. A waitress cleaned up the mess, gave me a smile and said, 'Don't worry Mr. Touhy, you can smash every sugar bowl in the place and everybody will understand.'"

As Touhy's luck would have it, that same week that he was released, Chicago hosted the National Conference of State Justices who had gathered in the Blackstone Hotel to discuss the encroaching power of the federal courts into their jurisdiction.

Barnes' ruling in the Touhy case was soundly condemned by these judges as a prime example of what they were talking about. It was their opinion that Federal Judge Barnes had overstepped his boundaries by hearing the Touhy case. They felt the issue should have remained on a state level. The Illinois State Attorney General's office agreed and filed a motion to have Roger returned to jail, arguing that Roger never challenged the aiding and abetting conviction in court and therefore accepted its terms. Johnstone would later argue that, at that point in 1943 when the aiding and abetting charge was added, Roger was financially strapped and unable to fight the case any farther.

It didn't matter, in the end the hearing judge held with the State of Illinois and issued a seizure writ directing the United States Marshal to arrest Touhy on sight.

A young reporter tracked Judge Barnes down to his farm and told him that his opinion on the Touhy case had been "reversed."

"Well, they can't do that, young man. They can't reverse my decision without a hearing."

The reporter, not really clear on the difference said, "Yeah, well, they did."

Word came to Roger Touhy while he was fishing at a resort in the Fox Lake area. He had just finished dinner when news came over the radio that a warrant had been issued for his arrest. Accompanied by Johnstone, he surrendered to federal marshals on a dark, rain filled day, just before 4:00 P.M. He had tasted freedom for less than forty-eight hours. He was rather stoic about the entire thing, almost as though he had come to expect the worst possible event as inevitable. "The fickle finger of fate," he said, "was going to give me another jab between the ribs."

He was taken from the Cook County jail at ten the next morning in a five-car motorcade consisting of fifteen heavily armed Chicago detectives and federal marshals. Officially they said they weren't expecting any trouble but had taken along the extra four cars "in case one of them breaks down or something."

Warden Ragen met Touhy at the Statesville Prison gates and said "Well, you're back."

Touhy smiled and said "Yeah. Not very long out."

Several hours later he was back to his old position, sweeping the jailhouse hallways as though nothing had happened.

Clara Touhy, her hair gone white, her face badly lined with age and worry, seemed to be in a state of shock over her husband's return to jail. "This is," she said, "a nightmare...this is all just a nightmare."

Freedom

A fter three years of exhausting legal maneuvering, in late 1957 Roger Touhy and Bob Johnstone stood before the State of Illinois Pardon and Parole Board and Roger told his story. When he was finished speaking, Benjamin Adamowski, the States Attorney for Cook County who had successfully tossed him back into Stateville on the aiding and abetting technicality, strode into the room and asked to be heard.

"My hopes sank," Touhy said, "...his words could condemn me."

But what Adamowski said surprised everyone. "My office has no objection to the release from prison of Mr. Touhy...in fact, I would urge it."

Eventually, and again with Robert Johnstone's help, Roger's 199-year term was reduced to three years on institutional parole, reducing his kidnapping sentence to six months. After that, he was to begin the commuted jail break sentence which was to expire April 27, 1961.

On November 13, 1959, Roger Touhy, a greying man of sixty-one, was paroled from prison after serving twenty-five years, nine months and thirteen days for a crime of which he was innocent. His health was gone and so was his money. He had been bled dry by the legal fees incurred from his seventeen denied petitions for freedom, which included four denials by the United States Supreme Court.

As he walked from the prison for the last time, he was draped in a gray overcoat that had been purchased for him in 1958 for his court appearances and a blue suit made in the prison tailor shop. He had the $600 which had remained on deposit in the prison before his 1942 escape.

Clara waited at the gates for him. They hugged for several minutes and whispered to each other through tears, and then walked, hand in hand, out of the prison. Bent and limping slightly, Touhy gave his first and last press conference on television as well as talking to print reporters at the Stateville guard house. He told the reporters that there was a gag order imposed on him. He disagreed with the order "since they didn't put one on Factor" but told reporters that he would have to be careful which questions he answered nonetheless.

There was an awkward silence for a moment which Roger broke. Referring to his first release several years before he said, "Any you guys get the feeling we've been through this before?"

That loosened things up.

He looked up at the grey skies and held his hand out to feel the mixture of light rain and snow falling around him.

"You know, it's funny. It was the same kind of day when I entered this place way back then."

"What are you going to do now, Mr. Touhy?"

"Please call me Roger...I've invented a lure for fresh water fishing; I'm going to manufacture it."

"Ever manufacture anything before, Rog?"

Touhy's eyes lit up. "Beer!"

"Do you hold any grudges, Mr. Touhy?"

"No. They have to live with their consciences."

"Who are they? Who do you mean by they?"

Johnstone leaned forward and whispered for his client not to reply.

"Roger, are you looking for Factor?"

"No. I'm not looking for anyone. I'm just going to take it easy for a while and see my wife and my two sons."

"Why did you lead the prison breakout?"

"I didn't plan it, I didn't lead it, I just went along."

"Did you learn anything in prison?"

"Nope. Not a goddamn thing."

Johnstone broke in "Well you learned patience, Roger."

Always a proud man, Roger fought back tears and said with a trembling chin, "You know, I never gave up hope that one day I would be standing here a free man."

He said he planned to move to Florida with his sons Roger Jr. and Tommy who were now in their mid-thirties with families of their own.

For the time being, he would live with his sister Ethel[11], who had made more than two thousand visits to her brother over the past quarter of a century and had appeared at seemingly endless hearings. During his internment she had worked her way, alone for the most part, through a maze of legal avenues in numerous attempts to free her brother from prison.

As he was driven back to Chicago in his nephew's cramped sports car, he thumbed through his personal belongings. There were two pictures drawn by his sons. He chuckled when he came across his 1942 draft card and a tiny black notebook with entries going back to 1919 when he was in the Navy. "I kept my telephone numbers and addresses of all my beer stops in code all through Prohibition. Nobody knew the code but me."

His color was pale and his hands shook as he thumbed through the book. Like his brothers, Roger suffered from the ravages of Parkinson's Disease, a degenerative disease of the nervous system then called "the shaking palsy."

As ordered, Roger went to the parole office in Chicago where he was given the details of the gag order he was under. Conversations with the media about the case were absolutely forbidden. An hour later, the ex-prisoner was dining on brisket of beef and hash brown potatoes in a west side restaurant with Ethel and Mike.[11] "Delicious, delicious" he muttered over and over again.

He would be dead within forty-nine hours.

---

11. Not their real names.

The Birth of Vegas and the Death of Tony "The Hat"

Tony Accardo, Chicago's new underworld boss, telephoned Johnny Rosselli, his man on the west coast, and told him he wanted him back in Chicago for a meeting at Meo's Restaurant with Murray Humpreys and Paul Ricca.

Always the hustler, Rosselli knew that the bosses were worried because they were losing what little presence they had in Las Vegas. As the self-declared power west of New York they felt, as a matter of mob pride, that they should have a major presence on the strip.

Rosselli filled them in on the situation at the Stardust. It was aimed at being, as he dubbed it, a "grind joint," a paradise for the low rollers, located right at the heart of the strip. If they wanted it, the bosses would have to pour a couple of hundred thousand dollars into the place to get it completed, but otherwise it was theirs. But first they had to deal with Tony Cornero, aka "Tony the Hat."

Las Vegas wasn't built by gangsters alone, and no matter how often it is written, Ben Siegel didn't build the first casino there, either. If any one hoodlum could take credit for inventing Las Vegas, it was Tony Cornero.

While it lasted, Cornero had an amazing life. He was born Anthony Cornero Stralla in an Italian village near the Swiss border in 1895. The Cornero family had owned a large farm there but his father lost it in a card game. More bad luck came when young Tony Cornero accidentally set fire to the family harvest, breaking them financially and forcing them to immigrate to San Francisco in the early 1920s.

At age sixteen, Tony pleaded guilty to robbery and did ten months in reform school. He moved to southern California and racked up another ten arrests in ten years which included three for bootlegging and three for attempted murder.

He was ambitious, but as late as 1922, Cornero was still driving a cab. Eventually he decided to branch off into the rum-running business. Starting with a string of small boats he smuggled high-priced whisky over the Canadian border and sold it to the better clubs in Los Angeles. At the same time, Cornero ran rum from Mexico to Los Angeles, his freighters easily avoiding the understaffed Coast Guard. Next, Tony purchased a merchant ship, the SS *Lily*, which he stocked with 4,000 cases of the best booze money could buy and ran the illicit alcohol into Los Angeles under cover of moonlight.

In 1931, Cornero decided to switch his effort to gambling. He and his brothers moved to Las Vegas and opened one of the town's first major casinos, the Green Meadows, which was known for its staff of attractive and friendly waitresses.

The Meadows turned a small, but healthy profit, and soon Cornero was investing his returns into other casinos in the state, mostly in Las Vegas. The money started to pour in and before long New York's Luciano, Lansky, and Frank Costello sent their representatives and demanded a cut of Cornero's action. Cornero who had always operated on the fringe of the national syndicate, refused to pay. Instead he had built up his own organization and was strong enough to turn the syndicate bosses down.

The syndicate, which had a small but powerful presence on the West Coast, prepared for war and started by burning Cornero's Green Meadows casino to the ground. Realizing he could never win the fight, Cornero sold out his interest in Nevada and returned to Los Angeles.

In 1938 Cornero bought several large ships and refurbished them into luxury casinos at a cost of more than $300,000. He anchored the ships three miles off the coast of Santa Monica and had gamblers shuttled from shore by way of motorboats. Cornero's lead ship, the *Rex*, had a crew of 350 waiters, waitresses, cooks, a full orchestra, and an entourage of enforcers. The first class dining room served superb French cuisine and on most nights some 2,000 patrons flooded onto the ship to gamble, dance and drink the night away. Tony was hauling in an estimated $300,000 a night after expenses, and the money would have continued to pour in had he not become the center of a reform movement in Los Angeles County.

State Attorney General Earl Warren ordered a raid on the *Rex* and several other of Cornero's off-coast ships. Cornero and the California government fought a series of battles, with Tony's lawyers arguing that his ships were operating in international waters, and the California government taking the indefensible stance that it didn't care where they were, they were still illegal.

Back and forth it went, until Cornero decided to fight back after raiders had smashed almost half a million dollars worth of gambling equipment on one of his ships,. When the law men came to raid his ships, Cornero ordered his men to repel the attackers with water hoses. A sea battle went on for nine hours and the lawmen finally gave up. But Cornero was beaten and he knew it; he closed his offshore operations.

Tony tried to open a few gambling houses inside Los Angeles, but Micky Cohen, the ruling bookie and drug dealer in the town, shut him down. When Cornero refused to back down, Cohen had his boys bomb Cornero's Beverly Hills estate. Fearing for his life, Cornero took his fortune and moved back to Las Vegas.

After several years in Vegas, Cornero undertook his dream to build the largest gambling casino-hotel in the world, the Stardust. To finance the construction of the Stardust Tony had borrowed $6,000,000 from the mob. As the casino neared completion Cornero couldn't account for half of the borrowed cash. The word on the street was that the bosses back east were whining that it had been a mistake to give him the money in the first place, because Tony the Hat was no businessman, just a dice jockey with high ambitions.

The truth is that the syndicate had probably set Tony up to fail from the very beginning. He never would have gotten a license to run the place because he had a long criminal record and an even longer list of powerful political enemies made across the state. And he had his enemies in the underworld as well. His endless arguments with the New York syndicates over the size of the Stardust—five hundred rooms—were legendary.

Meyer Lansky and Frank Costello were both positive that Las Vegas would never be able to attract enough gamblers to fill all of those rooms and the Stardust would cause a glut on the market, reducing prices for all the other casino rooms.

Cornero knew about the license problem, of course, but it didn't concern him. He believed he could get a license anyway. A few hundred grand went a long way in Nevada in the 1950s. But the word was that Moe Dalitz had already taken care of that and there was absolutely no way that Tony Cornero was going to get a gaming license in Nevada or anywhere else.

So, as the opening day drew closer, Cornero entered talks with Dalitz about leasing the place to the Dalitz operation. Dalitz was interested, but the terms that Cornero wanted were steep: a half a million a month. So Dalitz bided his time because he knew Cornero was broke and would have to come crawling back to him, and when he did they'd handle him.

As fate would have it, Tony not only helped build the Vegas that we know today but fittingly he died there, too. He dropped dead while gambling at the Desert Inn, with Moe Dalitz, the Godfather of Sin City, looking on with his fat arm draped around the waist of his slim and much younger wife.

Cornero had gone to the Desert Inn for a last chance meeting with Dalitz to beg the mob's favorite front man for financing to help him complete construction on his casino—the forever troubled Stardust. The place was scheduled to open in just two weeks, on July 13, 1955, and Cornero didn't have the cash to pay the staff or supply the house tables. He was in over his head—Dalitz and everybody else knew it

Cornero and Dalitz met for several long hours in a conference that went nowhere. Cornero wanted the mob's money and the mob wanted Cornero's casino. Neither party had any intention of giving anything to the other. During a break in the meeting, Cornero went out to the floor of the Desert Inn and gambled at the craps table and quickly fell into the hole for $10,000. Then a waitress came and handed him a tab for twenty-five dollars for the food and drinks he had. Cornero went ballistic. He was a guest of Moe Dalitz. The waitress didn't care; she wanted the money. Dalitz stood by and watched as Tony Cornero suffered through the ultimate insult to a big timer in Vegas.

Cornero screamed, ranted and raved and then grabbed his chest and fell forward on the table, desperately clutching his heart through his shirt, the dice still wrapped in his hands.

For decades the story circulated in the underworld that Cornero didn't die of a heart attack, that his drink had been poisoned. If he had been poisoned, the truth went with him to the grave. An autopsy was never performed. His body was shipped off to Los Angeles for a quick funeral where an organist from the Desert Inn knocked out a rendition of his favorite song, "The Wabash Cannonball Express" and eight hours after he hit the cold floor of the Desert Inn, Tony the Hat was eight feet under the ground.

Tony went out like the gambler he was. Of the estimated $25 million he had earned in his career as a gambler, Tony Cornero had less than $800 in his pockets when he died.

Nobody checked the contents of the drink he had been sipping before he dropped dead. No one cared enough to ask any serious questions. The important thing was that Tony Cornero was dead. Jake the Barber Factor, a Chicago favorite, was moved into position as the Stardust's new owner of record, and everybody in mobdom was happy.

Well, everybody except Tony Cornero.

A few weeks after Tony's death, Jake the Barber announced that he had just purchased the Stardust.

20 Jake the Barber— Innkeeper

fter Roger Touhy was tried and convicted of kidnapping him, life for Jake the Barber remained interesting. He got involved in some questionable oil leases in Arkansas and had settled a federal income tax charge against him with a cash payment of $120,000, but otherwise life was good.

However, trouble was never far from Factor and on August 22, 1942, Jake the Barber and eleven others were indicted by an Iowa grand jury for their part in the whisky swindle that conned a total of $459,000 out of some 300 victims in a twelve-state area.

Factor was tried and found guilty.

On February 3, 1943, the court was called to order. Judge John Bell—the same Judge who had heard the Hamm kidnapping case a decade before— sentenced Factor to ten years at hard labor plus a $10,000 fine. When Factor heard the sentence, he dropped down in his chair and covered his head as if the ceiling were falling in on him. His attorney, Thomas McMeeken, one of Roger Touhy's lawyers at the Hamm trial, had to pull Factor up to his feet so the court could continue reading the sentence. While the judge was in mid-sentence, Factor broke down and begged loudly for the judge to listen to him. All he wanted, he said, was not to go to jail. He sobbed through the rest of the proceedings. When asked by the court if he had anything else to say, Factor nodded his head and muttered something unintelligible through his tears.

When he gained control of himself, he whimpered something about how he had helped the government put away the Touhy gang and how he feared for his life. His story fell on deaf ears. No one wanted to hear about threats on Factor's life from a gangster grown old and gray long ago; there was no Tubbo Gilbert or States Attorney's Office around to run interference for him. Jake the Barber was going to prison.

• • •

Factor was released from Sandstone Prison in February of 1948. He was sentenced to parole for the remaining four years of his ten-year sentence. In 1954, at the end of his parole sentence, he told the parole board he was broke. In 1955, one year after his final meeting with the parole board, and six years since he last held a job, convicted felon John Factor announced that he had purchased the Stardust Casino in Las Vegas. Jake the Barber was now the owner and operator of one of the largest casinos in the world.

It was Murray Humpreys who decided that Jake the Barber would buy the Stardust with the only explanation out of the mob being that "Jake owes Chicago a big one."

Humpreys must have put up the money to buy the casino. From that point on, Jake the Barber was

Chicago's front man in the Stardust, and it was a mob gold mine.

At first the outfit was excited at the prospect of having John Factor as its head man. He was, at least by mob standards, trustworthy. He was smart enough to know the outfit would kill him in a heartbeat if he tried anything creative.

The problem with Factor was that he, like Cornero, couldn't get a liquor license. As Hank Messick wrote, "...much to the disgust of the Chicago boys. The Barber tried everything he could to get a license but there was no way it was going to happen. He finally bowed to reality and announced that he would lease to the Desert Inn Group....It took a western Appalachian to solve the matter."

In a meeting held in mob lawyer Sidney Korshak's Beverly Hills office, Meyer Lansky, Longy Zwillman, Doc Stacher (representing New York and New Jersey), Moe Dalitz and Morris Kleinman decided that Dalitz would lease the casino operation. Dalitz represented the Desert Inn. All involved agreed that Dalitz's Desert Inn would pay $100,000 a month—a low figure for the second largest money maker in Las Vegas—to operate the casino part of the Stardust. Factor would, at least on paper, still own the building, the grounds and the hotel operation.

Dalitz, who was one of the founding members of the national crime syndicate, would run the day-to-day operation and Johnny Rosselli—Brian Foy's old pal—would be off in the shadows, representing the true owners of the Stardust: Paul Ricca, Tony Accardo, Sam Giancana and Murray Humpreys.

Everybody was making money off the Stardust. Carl Thomas, the master of the Las Vegas skim, estimated that the Chicago mob was skimming $400,000 a month from the Stardust in the early sixties, and that was only for the one arm bandits. Blackjack, craps, keno, roulette and poker yielded a different skim.

It was more money then they had ever dreamed of and nothing, absolutely nothing, was going to prevent them from taking it.

And then Roger Touhy was released from prison.

Roger Touhy Must Die

The ringleaders of those who were making money hand-over-fist at the Stardust in the early sixties had all grown out of the old-time Chicago syndicate. Virtually all of them had been players in Capone's mob and its war against the Touhy organization.

When Roger entered prison in 1934, there was some question as to whether the Chicago syndicate, then under Frank Nitti's control, would make it into the next decade. The end of prohibition had taken away its beer money. Additionally, the Great Depression, which hit Chicago extremely hard, had hurt its traditional rackets like white slavery and prostitution. To top it off, the war with Touhy for control over labor unions had cost them dearly.

But when Touhy was defeated, Nitti did take control over most of Chicago's labor unions and even joined the New York and New Jersey mob in an ill-fated move on the Hollywood entertainment locals. That collapsed in 1942, when federal indictments locked up virtually all of the leaders of the Chicago mob. The indictments even caused Frank Nitti to fire a bullet through his own brain. But by 1959 the

mob was under the firm leadership of Paul Ricca—
the man who had murdered Matt Kolb—and Tony
Accardo, who was just a small-time hood when
Touhy had been locked away.

For appearances anyway, the outfit's official
leader was Sam "Momo" Giancana, a merciless thug
who had fought the Touhys as part of the 42 Gang
under Rocco DeGrazio's command back in 1932.

But Giancana was nothing more then a lightning
rod to keep the government away from Accardo and
Ricca. The fact was that Accardo was the boss. In
fact, he remains to this day the most powerful, successful and respected boss known by the Chicago
syndicate, or probably any other criminal syndicate
for that matter. He also had the distinction of being
the mob leader with the longest-lived career. During
his tenure, Accardo's power was long-reaching and
frightfully vast.

He was so respected and feared in the national
mafia that in 1948 when he declared himself the
arbitrator for any mob problems west of Chicago—
in effect proclaiming all of that territory as his—no
one in the syndicate argued.

He was the boss pure and simple. Unlike Torrio,
Nitti or Ricca, Tony Accardo looked exactly like what
he was—a mob thug who could and did dispatch
men and women to their death over money or disre-
spect. He was a self-professed peasant. But he was
a reserved man and a thinker, unlike Colosimo,
Capone, Giancana and all those who came after
Giancana.

Unlike the other bosses, Accardo knew his limitations. He consulted often with Ricca, Murray the
Camel Humpreys and Short Pants Campagna
because he recognized their intelligence and wisdom
and liked to use it.

He admitted lacking the crafty thinking ability of Ricca, Nitti or Torrio and the flair and self deprecating wit of Capone or Giancana. Despite his shortcomings, it was Accardo who expanded the outfit's activities into new rackets after the end of the prohibition era. It was Accardo who, recognizing the dangers of the white slave trade, streamlined the old prostitution racket during the war years into the new call girl service which was copied by New York families even though they laughed at the idea at first.

Two decades after prohibition was repealed Accardo introduced bootlegging to the dry states of Kansas and Oklahoma, flooding them with illegal whisky. He moved the outfit into slot and vending machines, counterfeiting cigarette and liquor tax stamps and expanding narcotics smuggling on a worldwide basis.

Watching someone as clever as Paul Ricca and as smart as Frank Nitti go to jail over the Bioff scandal, Accardo pulled the organization away from labor racketeering and extortion. Under Accardo's reign the Chicago mob exploded in growth and became increasingly wealthy.

The outfit grew because aside from the Kefauver committee, there wasn't a focused attempt on the part of any law enforcement agency to break it up. The FBI was busy catching Cold War spies and denied that the Mafia or even organized crime existed at all.

Under Accardo's leadership, the gang set its flag in Des Moines, Iowa; downstate Illinois; Southern California; Kentucky; Las Vegas; Indiana; Arizona; St. Louis, Missouri; Mexico; Central and South America. Accardo's long reign highlighted a golden era for the Chicago syndicate. But it also ushered in the near collapse of the outfit as well. In 1947, as Tony Accardo took the reigns of power from Paul Ricca, the outfit produced an estimated $300 million in business per year, with Accardo, Humpreys, Ricca and Giancana taking in an estimated forty to fifty million each per year.

Accardo pensioned off the older members of the mob and gave more authority to its younger soldiers, mostly former 42 Gang members like Sam Giancana, the Battaglias and Marshal Ciafano.

The money poured in. Hundreds of thousands of dollars rolled in everyday from all points where Chicago ruled. The hoods who had survived the shootouts, gang wars, purges, cop shootings, national exposés and the federal and state investigations now saw rewards for what they had so dilligently hustled for.

By 1959, the Chicago outfit was stealing millions of dollars from the Teamsters' pension fund, which they had more or less turned into their own piggy bank. The outfit was pouring much of that money into Las Vegas casinos, including The Stardust which Jake the Barber fronted.

It was all so easy, and then Roger Touhy announced that he intended to pursue a $300,000,000 lawsuit against John Factor and all the others—Ricca, Humpreys, Accardo—who had helped railroad him to prison for twenty-five years.

The bosses, Ricca and Accardo, watched and worried. They thought they had buried Touhy alive in Statesville but Johnstone got him out. This proved to the syndicate that Touhy's lawyer was no hack. When he sued, he meant business.

Worse yet, the word on the street was that Touhy was working with Ray Brennan, an investigative reporter for the *Chicago Tribune*. Brennan was somebody to worry about. He knew what he was doing and he was honest. Brennan kept turning up asking the wrong questions about Teamster loans to the Stardust.

The way Ricca and Accardo saw it, there was only one answer. Roger Touhy had to die.

A few days before Roger was released from prison, retired Rabbi Harry Zinn walked the few blocks from his home to the rental apartment building he owned, directly across the street from Roger's sister's house.

Zinn was there because one of his tenants said that she had seen a rough-looking man loitering in the building over the past several days and the Rabbi should come over and investigate. He walked around the property and then went down into the building's basement to check the boilers. As he rounded a corner in the dark cellar, he spotted a rough-looking man, with a dark complexion, staring out of a basement window at Touhy's sister's house. Zinn noted the expensive fur-lined tan-colored winter waist coat and knew it wasn't a street bum who had come in out of the cold.

Sensing Zinn's presence the man spun around, glared at the old rabbi and said, "What are you doing here?"

Zinn asked, "Who are you?"

The stranger was flushed. "I'm just checking on my kid, my son, he's running around with some broad in this neighborhood."

Even as he spoke, the stranger was walking toward Zinn and then suddenly brushed past him, almost knocking the old man over as he ran up the stairs to the front door of the building with Zinn in pursuit. By the time Zinn made it to the street, the stranger had disappeared. If the hit men had learned anything from watching Ethel's house, it was that killing Roger Touhy wouldn't be easy. The old bootlegger had taken precautions. He refused to leave home unless he had one of his two "watchdogs," as he called them, with him, and both of those watchdogs were cops.

Ethel's son, Mike, was a twenty-three-year-old policeman and part-time law student who traveled around town with his uncle when time allowed.

The other problem was the other cop—Walter J. Miller—then sixty-two years old. Back in 1932, Tubbo Gilbert assigned Miller to guard Factor for three months after Jake appeared on the streets of LaSalle.

So if they were going to kill Touhy, they would probably have to kill one of the two cops with him, the old one would be easier, but if they had to kill the young one, well so be it. But still, even for the Chicago outfit, cop killing was more or less a forbidden act. Touhy's suit threatened the whole casino operation and his death warranted bringing down the risk of killing a cop.

Roger never feared for his life; that wasn't why he had the two men travel with him. "If I have Mike and Walter with me," he told Ray Brennan, "they won't be able to pin a phoney parole violation on me. They'll never hit me. They'll try to frame me for a parole violation probably, but they'll never hit me."

• • •

December 1959 would be Roger's first Christmas as a free man in twenty-five years and he was upbeat despite the reality facing him. His health was gone and so was his money. His two sons had matured without a father. He was virtually a stranger to them and his wife of almost four decades was in fragile health.

The state parole board refused to lift the gag order placed on him after he told the board that he wanted to go on the record and reply to the charges that Factor was making against him in the press. The Board told him he would have to wait for at least another year before they would lift the gag. But they also told Touhy that they didn't care what he said about Factor. The gag order wasn't about protecting Factor, it was about protecting the State of Illinois from looking stupid and corrupt for tossing innocent men in jail.

Despite his failing health and depleted bank account, Roger began to prepare to face John Factor in court. This was no easy chore. Factor had grown rich, very rich, over the years. Apart from his interests in the Stardust, he had considerable holdings in real estate, commercial insurance and stocks, and with that kind of war chest behind him, Factor could afford the best legal talent in the world. To prove it, Factor was suing Touhy and Ray Brennan, his collaborator, for libel over *The Stolen Years*, the book Roger had written about his life, claiming that it injured his reputation as a civic leader and philanthropist.

Roger had used his spare time while in prison to write his life story. After a first draft, he decided that he would need a professional writer's help and called in Ray Brennan. Brennan was the archetype of the tough-edged, hard-drinking, newsman with a heart as big as the city he loved so much. A midwestern Irishman, he got his first big break in 1933 when Arthur Brisbane, the most influential editor in the Hearst newspaper empire, went to the Cook County jail to interview Al Capone. Capone told Brisbane that if he were released, he would help find the Lindbergh baby. Brisbane sat on the story and the next morning Capone spotted Brennan walking through the jail and said, "Hey kid, you want a good story?" Brennan took Capone's story and ran with it. The Hearst organization followed with Brisbane's story a day later and Brennan was the new star crime reporter in Chicago. A while later, when John Dillinger escaped from the Crown Point jail, Brennan called the jail just to check with the warden.

"So how's your star prisoner doing?" Brennan asked.

"Well, I don't know," came the jailers reply, "'cause that slippery son of bitch just escaped."

Brennan kept all of the jail's lines tied up and grabbed the year's best exclusive story.

Brennan had sat through the Hamm and Factor kidnapping trials, fascinated by the characters involved. Later he would write several stories about the case which brought him to Touhy's eye. What intrigued Touhy about Brennan was his relentless pursuit of the classified testimony that Tubbo Gilbert had given to the Kefauver committee when it arrived in Chicago in 1950. That year, Gilbert— who was still the central power behind the States Attorney's Office—was a candidate for Cook County Sheriff. He began his campaign despite the fact that most Chicago crime reporters considered him a full-fledged member of the syndicate—one who answered directly to Murray Humpreys.

Fascinated with Gilbert, Brennan wrote:

Gilbert's name came up during the hearings and he was requested, as opposed to ordered, to testify before the committee, which he did but from behind closed doors, a most unusual thing and the transcript was later impounded.

Since it was just before the election and

Kefauver was a good Democrat he agreed to the terms that Tubbo Gilbert had set up.

Gilbert was questioned for two hours behind closed doors. When it was over Estes Kefauver gave a briefing that left more questions than answers.

Brennan tried everything he could to find out what Gilbert had told the Committee, but was unsuccessful and had more or less given up and retired to his favorite watering hole for a drink "when inspiration struck." He flew to Washington, posed as a member of the committee's staff, went to the stenographer's office saying that he had dropped by to pick up a copy of "some guy named Gilbert's testimony."

Remarkably, they handed him a bound copy of Gilbert's secret testimony. Gilbert's statements before the committee were riveting. He admitted to gambling in mob-run joints while enforcing the city's no gambling laws. He also admitted winning more than $7,000 in 1948, by wagering on football, baseball, prize fights and elections. His wealth was estimated to be in the millions[12]—an amazing savings accomplishment for a civil servant who never earned more than $40,000 in one year.

Gilbert admitted to the committee that it was true that his personal records were missing from the police department and that he was a frequent guest of gangster Owney Madden in Hot Springs. The most shocking admission was that while he was in charge of the States Attorney's Office, justice was doled out on a "cash and carry basis."

The Kefauver committee secretly concluded that Tubbo Gilbert's administration when he was Chicago's top cop, "was neglect of official duty and

---

12. He would later deny this figure, instead estimating his own worth at "just over $300,000."

shocking indifference to violations of the law."

The Sun Times printed the testimony that Brennan dug up and Cook County voters turned out in record numbers for an off-year election to vote against Tubbo Gilbert. His opponent won by a remarkable 400,000 votes. A few days later, Gilbert retired from office and announced that he would take a position as chief of security at Arlington and Washington race tracks where his brother Maurice was a lieutenant. The Gilbert story continued to unravel when Brennan discovered that though Maurice Gilbert was drawing a salary from the track, he had officially been out on sick leave from the Chicago police department since 1948. After that, Gilbert packed up his millions and moved to California where he said he planned to open a detective agency in Los Angeles. Shortly after arriving in Los Angeles he suffered a heart attack and went into semi-retirement.

Tubbo Gilbert never held a grudge against Brennan for bringing him down. In fact, in one of Tubbo Gilbert's last tirades against the Chicago press, he jabbed his finger into a reporter's chest and barked, "All of you are a pack of rats. The only one of youse who has any class at all is Ray Brennan...and he's a rat too." Brennan understood the back-handed compliment.

President Harry Truman, however, did hold a grudge. He threw a fit over the Democratic party's loss in Illinois, and he held Brennan responsible. As a result Brennan was indicted for posing as a federal official and, if convicted, he could have been sentenced to six years for stealing the transcript. The Justice Department brought him before several federal hearings, actually handcuffing him once, before it dropped the case with the ruling that his actions had "no criminal intent as we generally understand it."

Roger Touhy had followed this entire story from jail. After the case against Brennan was dropped Touhy wrote to him and asked him if he wanted to help write his life story. This brought about the $3,000,000 libel suit from Jake the Barber.

Anatomy of a Hit

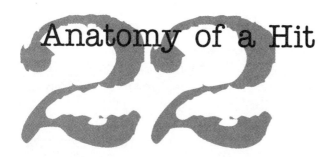

"In a world where there are few roses, Roger Touhy never pretended to be one but his finish emphasizes that even a man who was not so good may be the victim of men who are worse."

—*Chicago Sun Times*

In the early evening of the night he died, Roger Touhy prepared to drive to a meeting at the Chicago Press Club with Ray Brennan and their book publisher to discuss Factor's suit against them.

At the same time, across town, John Factor dined at the Singapore Steak House on Rush street. The place was owned by two old saloon keepers named Fritzel and Jacobson, whom Jake had known from Prohibition days. Tommy Downs managed the restaurant which was popular with the mob in the 1950s. Downs was once in charge of security at the Sportsman Park Race Track which was previously owned by Bugs Moran and later by Frank Nitti. In 1959 the Singapore Steak House was secretly owned by Chuckie English, a former member of the 42 Gang and right-hand man of Sam Giancana, and it remained one of Chicago's celebrity hangouts despite the mob connections.

Jake said he had flown in from Los Angeles to spend the holidays with his son Jerome and to press his suit against Touhy and Brennan over *The Stolen Years.*

Also seen in the Singapore that night was Murray Humpreys, who had helped Factor rig his own kidnapping almost three decades before. As always, Humpreys sat with a glass of whisky in front of him. The Hump put it there to impress the others and nothing more, since he never drank.

During the rest of the evening, the normally low profile Humpreys made sure of accounting for his whereabouts. He left the Singapore and strolled down Clark Street where he was seen at Fritzels, a fashionable restaurant and later at L'Escarot, another restaurant, returning home he said at 3:00 A.M.

Tubbo Gilbert left his palatial homes in Los Angeles and Palm Springs where he lived in semi-retirement, and was in town overseeing his extensive real estate and contracting interests. He would later tell reporters that he had flown into Chicago to spend the holidays with his grandchildren.

At 5:00 P.M. sharp, Walter Miller pulled his car up to the front of Roger's sister's home to take Touhy to his meeting with Brennan and the publisher. At 5:55, they pulled into the Sheraton Towers Hotel garage and took the elevator to the top floor to the wood-paneled press club. Brennan, customary scotch in hand, greeted them at the door. They hung up their winter coats and walked to a round table in the middle of the room where Richard H. Brown, a New York lawyer representing the book's publisher, Pennington Press, was seated.

Brennan ordered appetizers and a German beer

for Touhy. They talked for three hours about the book. It was a grim conversation. Factor's suit had hurt the book's sales because the big chain department stores fearing a suit from Factor, refused to carry it. As if that wasn't bad enough the Teamsters had refused to load and carry copies on their trucks.

At 9:15 Miller said they had to leave because Roger was on an 11:00 P.M. curfew. Brennan helped his two guests on with their topcoats. Miller's coat sagged from the heavy .38 caliber in his right pocket.

The last thing Touhy said to Brennan was, "Factor goes around calling me every vile name in the book. I'm going to Springfield on Friday to ask Governor Stratton for a full pardon. Goodnight, kid."

Miller drove quickly to Touhy's sister's house. He was worried about making the curfew so he didn't take the precaution of driving around the block as he usually did. They were running late and it was a bitter eight degrees outside with an ugly wind whipping across the street.

He parked and the two men slowly walked up the six steps of Ethel's porch, Miller's hulking frame towering over the limping and bent Touhy. The only sound that could be heard was the occasional passing traffic on Washington Boulevard a half a block away. Then Roger heard a call from one of two men running toward him. "Wait, hold on, we're police officers!"

Roger and Miller turned their heads as one. Instinctively, Miller reached for his service revolver but it was too late. The men were running toward them, leveling their shotguns as they sprinted across the frozen street. With a policeman's eye, Miller noticed that one of the killers stood at least six feet tall. He was wearing a topcoat. The other was perhaps three inches shorter. Miller aimed at him and fired.

The killers fired back. Miller raised his left arm to cover his face and nearly had it blown off at the elbow. Dozens of pellets lodged into his back and legs. The transom over the door was shredded by shot pellets and the vibration from the blasts had shattered the glass in the front door.

Before the blasts knocked him to the ground, Miller was able to get off a total of five shots. Two shots landed in the windshield of a car parked on the opposite side of the street, two more grounded themselves into the front lawn and one found its way into the leg of one of the assassins.[13]

Almost at the exact moment that Miller was blown backward, two huge blasts from the killers' shotguns knocked Roger across the porch and then smashed him face first into the ground. Pellets tore a hole in Touhy's inner left leg, the other pellets dug into his right upper rib cage. His leg was barely attached to his body.[14]

In all, the killers fired at least seven blasts with their shotguns and probably three more with an automatic pistol and then they were gone.

The murder had taken less than forty-five seconds.

Miller crawled over to Touhy and said, "Say an act of contrition, Rog."

---

13. Several days later, reporter Sandy Smith went to the home of Sam Giancana and interviewed the crime boss about the killing.

The Chicago Police had been telling reporters that they "were searching high and low" for Giancana, to question him about the Touhy murder, but were unable to find him.

Smith, who interviewed Giancana on his front lawn, noted that the gangster's foot was wrapped in bandages and he limped.

It's possible that Giancana, a former 42 Gang member who was noted for his fantastic driving skills, may have been the third gunman that Miller saw and Touhy hadn't seen. Miller reported that he shot at least one of the gunmen and heard him scream out "Son of bitch!"

14. Police officer Daniel Stillwagon said later, "They blew that guy apart; you could see that the leg was just hanging on by some veins and some skin."

Ethel was in the kitchen drying the dinner dishes when she heard the blasts. She had been half listening for her brother's footsteps on the front porch, but when she heard the blasts, she knew he was dead. She had been expecting it.

She ran out to the front steps and saw Roger, twitching violently in a massive pool of his and Miller's blood.

She bent down over her brother and tried to pick up his head.

Roger held her hand and moaned, "It was two cops."

Patrolmen Robert Peters, Henry Sullivan and Daniel Stillwagon were the first on the scene. They didn't try to stop the blood because it didn't seem possible. Their only thought was to rush Touhy to a hospital.

Two ambulances were called, but there wasn't enough time to wait; Peters could see that Touhy was bleeding to death in front of his eyes.

When a third squad car pulled up, Peters placed Roger in the back seat and drove him to nearby Saint Anne's hospital.

Miller, who was conscious but in agony, volunteered to wait for an ambulance and told the cops to get Roger to a hospital.

Peters rode in the back seat with Touhy, holding his hand and making a valiant but hopeless effort to stop the gush of blood from the gaping holes in the dying old man's legs.

Roger kept nodding his head at the cop and saying, "I'm all right, I'm okay."

But he wasn't. He was losing too much blood from the shotgun pellets drilled into his leg, in the place where his knee had been just a few minutes before. They arrived at the emergency room at 10:35 P.M. where a shock trauma team headed by Dr.

Patrick Vitullo placed Roger under an oxygen tent and wheeled him into an operating room.

Dr. Vitullo applied a tourniquet to the upper portions of Touhy's legs in a fruitless effort to stop the bleeding just as Chief of Detectives John Archer stepped into the room, slipping and almost falling to the floor that was slippery with Touhy's blood.

Dr. Vitullo leaned over Roger's face to check his breathing.

"Mr. Touhy, who shot you?"

"Two men."

"Do you know them?"

"No."

"Where is your identification?"

"I never carry any."

"Do you have any money on you?"

"About $200.00."

"Where is it?"

"Right front pocket."

Then he faded.

"Mr. Touhy, you must try to stay awake."

There was no reply. A nurse rifled through Roger's bloody pants' pockets and found $240, a pack of non-filtered cigarettes, a pair of reading glasses and two drawings from his sons, done twenty-six years before.

The doctor worked frantically, but knew his patient would never survive the massive loss of blood. Father Richard Birmingham was brought into the room and gave Roger Touhy the last rites of the Catholic Church which he completed at 11:23 P.M. Two minutes later, at 11:25, Roger Touhy expired.

Ray Brennan came into the emergency room just as the nurse pressed down Roger's eyelids for the final time and pulled the sheet up over his head. "Rotten bastards," he whispered over and again.

The killing shook Chicago and the question all

over town was "Why?"...Why kill a rumpled, half-crippled old man? Why, as *Newsweek* put it, kill the "not so Terrible Touhy"?

Nobody in Chicago really wanted an answer, but they had to make it look as though they did. By now, 701 mob murders later, going through the motions of showing outrage, was standard practice.

Mayor Daly was awakened by his aides who told him that Roger Touhy had been killed. Daly climbed out of bed and ordered Police Commissioner O'Connor to personally investigate the killing.

O'Connor ordered his police to pick up Marshal Ciafano and Sam Teets Battaglia. Ciafano and Battaglia were the mob's favorite hit men, both were former 42 Gang members who had fought against Touhy in 1932, and both had been arrested by Walter Miller a few years before on armed robbery charges.

Marshal Ciafano was found at the Trade Winds bar by detectives who dragged him screaming, off his bar stool and carried him by his arms and legs to a waiting squad car, tossed him into the back seat and drove him to police headquarters for questioning.

They found Battaglia in his expensive home in Oak Park and hauled him in for questioning but then let him go.

Neither Paul Ricca, Tony Accardo, Murray Humpreys[15] nor Sam Giancana were ever questioned for their role in Touhy's murder.

---

15. A recently declassified FBI document reveals that on January 28, 1960, Humpreys discussed Touhy's killing with labor goon Joey Glimco. The informant who reported the conversation said it was conducted mostly in whispers. Suspecting that he would be arrested by the U.S. Treasury, which was investigating Touhy's murder, for his role in the killing, Humpreys said, "Dirty bastards, if I ever want to dispute them, I didn't keep it all to myself, see?...I figure, if they're gonna get real hot on me, they want to fuck with me like they did on that shit, they're not gonna give me shit. So, I just keep still, 'cause I got the answers for them.....

He also added that, "He (Touhy?) was dying a long time ago. He was on a stretcher, you know?"

Several days after the murder, John Factor testified at the coroner's inquest with an enormous diamond ring glittering from his pinky finger. Police ushered him into a waiting room where Ethel sat in a corner with Tommy Touhy Jr., her face buried in a Persian lamb coat, her eyes hidden by dark glasses. The room was small. Factor, always amiable, turned to the Touhys and nodded and smiled. They glared at him. Then he realized who they were. He turned his face to the wall and waited for police officers to move him to another room.

Before he left Chicago for Los Angeles, Factor was allowed to take a lie detector test to prove his innocence. This was the same type of test Touhy wasn't allowed to take to prove his own innocence more than twenty-four years earlier. Chief of Detectives Archer watched the test being administered and announced to the press mob waiting on the street, "Factor had nothing to do with the shooting and no knowledge of the participants or the reasons. We have no further reasons to question him."

Reporters tracked down Tubbo Gilbert who met them with his standard, "I have no comment," but then, as always, he talked anyway; "I have no idea who would want to do this either."

Perhaps not realizing the blatant stupidity of the question, Tubbo asked "I'll say this, if Touhy was so innocent, why did he need a bodyguard?"

Roger's body traveled from the Alexian Brothers Hospital to the Cook County Morgue—the same route that John Dillinger's and Frank Gusenberg's gunned down bodies had taken back in 1936.

While Touhy's dead body was waiting for transport to the morgue, a scant two blocks from his childhood home on South Robie Street, a photographer snapped a photo of the corpse, his face frozen in terror and pain, the mouth pried open in one last frantic breath for life.

Roger's grief-stricken sister was left with the awful task of identifying her brother's body a few hours later.

The next morning, at 8:30 A.M., a solitary hearse bearing Touhy's body in its coffin, slowly pulled out of the back alley of the funeral parlor. It was decided Touhy would be buried at the family grave at Chicago's Boot Hill Cemetery, Mount Carmel. Not far from his gravesite were the tombs of Dion O'Bannion, Frank Nitti, the Genna Brothers, Paul "Needle Nose" La Briola, Al Capone and by 1992, Tony Accardo. The tombstone would bear the name TOWEY, the Anglo-Irish spelling of his family name, in the northwest corner of the burial ground where his brothers Johnny, Joe, James and Eddie were entombed.

Secrecy surrounded the funeral. Chief of Detectives Archer, who had been planning an observation detail for the funeral which he expected to take place the following week, was caught completely off guard and was told about it by a *Chicago Tribune* reporter.

Arriving at the site only minutes after the coffin, Archer watched from the warmth of his car as Clara and her sons, Roger Jr. and Tommy, stood in the bitter winter cold while the funeral director recited Roman Catholic prayers over the coffin. Nearby, six workmen stood by with their shovels at ready. There were no other mourners, no flowers, no pallbearers. The service ended in seven minutes and a weeping Clara was led away to a car by Tommy. A freezing wind picked up and swept across the yard as the workmen lowered Roger Touhy's coffin in its grave.

Archer walked up to the gravesite and one of the workmen paused from shoveling dirt and asked, "Is it true they only gave him twenty-eight days of freedom?"

Archer nodded, that it was.

"That hardly seems enough," the workman said. "Just doesn't seem right."

Epilogue:
The Pardon

I n 1962, just two days before he was to be deport-
ed from the United States to a jail cell in
England, John Factor was granted a
Presidential Pardon by John F. Kennedy.

• • •

Shortly after Roger Touhy was out of the way, the
Chicago mob saw fit to push Factor out of the
Stardust casino and place the operation into the
steady hands of Moe Dalitz. But when the facts
behind the transaction hit the media—that John
Factor had sold one of the largest and most profitable casinos in the world for the paltry sum of $15
milllion—Attorney General Robert Kennedy
ordered an investigation into the sale. The United
States Internal Revenue Service along with the
State of Nevada Gaming Commission started a joint
investigation into the Stardust sale.

The joint force intended to call Factor in for questioning. However they were beaten to the punch
when the Los Angeles Office of the Immigration and
Naturalization Service (INS) suddenly ordered him
in to to show due cause why he shouldn't be deported to England where he was still a wanted felon.
The INS had now decided, based on Jake's arrest
and conviction in 1942 for fraud, that he was an

undesirable alien. At seventy years of age, John Factor, who had lived in America since at least 1919, was being ordered out of the country.

The problem was that the INS had never closed its record on Factor since he entered the country through Mexico after the British stock swindle. It was a minor, white lie that kept the record open. Jake had told the INS at the border that he had been born in England while their records said he was born in Poland and the INS could prove it. Unable to show due cause why he shouldn't be deported, Factor was ordered to surrender to the INS on December 25, 1962, at which point he would be arrested and deported to Poland.

At the time, Poland was a backward, war-torn country, crushed under the iron-fisted rule of the Russian Communist Party. The conditions in Poland caused Factor to fight hard to prove to the government that he was, in fact, a British citizen. The problem with sending Jake to Britain was that his conviction for stock fraud remained in force. The second he landed at Heathrow, he'd be jailed. Adding to Factor's woes was the ongoing IRS investigation into payment of his back taxes for the years 1935 through 1939. The government wanted Factor to explain where he received $479,093.27 in income, and Factor couldn't remember. If he was deported, the Government would impound his holdings, which Factor estimated to be $13 million, until the matter was settled, which meant that he would leave the country the way he came in, penniless.[16]

The only thing that could save Factor from deportation was death or a miracle. The miracle came straight from the White House in the form of a pardon.

---

16. If his wife, Rella, went with him, he would have been more fortunate; the INS estimated her wealth to be, in 1960, $40 million.

Presidential pardons, the last imperial power of the Executive Office, have long been the golden parachute for the mob's monied elite looking to avoid deportation, obtain a position in the casino business or a labor union, or to help muscle their way into a legitimate enterprise.

Abusing the pardon privilege has had a torrid and often astounding history, even on a state level. In the early 1920s, Illinois' incredibly corrupt Governor, Len Small, sold an estimated 500 pardons before he was indicted and chased from office. Small's broker on the pardon deals was a union extortionist named "Umbrella Mike" Boyle, a bigwig in the Electrical Workers Union. Among Boyle's clients was Spike O'Donnell, who started the great Chicago beer wars of 1926 upon his release.

In the 1970s, when federal prosecutors tried to deport southwestern Pennsylvania mob boss, John S. LaRocca, Governor John Fine pardoned the alleged godfather of corruption along with his capo, Frank Rosa. Later, Governor George Earle pardoned Mafia bosses Joe Luciano, Luigi Quaranta and alleged Capporeime Nicholas Piccolo. He also pardoned Frank "Binkie" Palermo, allegedly a made member of the Mafia; Felix Bocchiccio, a fight fixer; Leo Kamminski and Louie Barish, suspected mob members.

One of the most outrageous pardons on record belongs to Harry Truman who pardoned "Ice Pick" Danny Motto, a labor thug in the Gambino family. He had been convicted of wartime racketeering and as a result, Danny the Ice Pick wasn't allowed to hold an "elective" office in New York's Bakers Union local 350, a 900-member local which he terrorized from 1939 until his death in the 1980s. Motto's 1947 federal racketeering charge, plus a previous one for murder, gave the Justice Department due cause to deport him.

However, at the last moment, after deportation had been ordered, Truman granted a pardon and the deportation was canceled. The man who worked behind the scenes on Motto's behalf was his lawyer, Herb Itkin. Itkin was a shadowy figure with unspecified connections to Naval Intelligence and later to the CIA. It was Itkin who introduced New York's mayoral administration (under John Lindsay) to labor mobster and loan shark Anthony "Tony Ducks" Corralo, who was also Danny Motto's boss. That meeting would eventually lead to the James Marcus scandal of 1966.

Truman also pardoned many felons from the Boss Pendergast political machine. More than half of those pardoned were convicted of interfering with a citizen's right to vote, or, in other words, were members of Owney Madden's goon squads.

And now it was John F. Kennedy's turn. During his brief presidency, Kennedy issued 472 pardons, more than any chief executive before or since. About half of these appear to be questionable, at best.

On November 26, 1962, Attorney General Robert Kennedy did something unusual: he changed the laws that govern presidential pardons. It was unusual because the fourteen sets of rules, all advisory in nature, that govern presidential pardons, have seldom been tampered with, since they were written in 1893.

The change that Kennedy made in the rules,[17]

---

17. The rules that govern federal pardons, are just that...rules...not laws. They can be made, broken or ignored by the President. All of these rules are simply procedural in nature.

Pardons are the last imperial power of the presidency, and aside from the few pardons that have outraged Americans, such as Jimmy Hoffa's highly questionable pardon, the practice goes on, unregulated.

only sixteen days before John Factor was pardoned, allowed all pardon requests to go directly to the White House and then to the Justice Department, and not the other way around.

A few days after Kennedy changed the rules for pardons, an alcoholic Chicago hood named Chuckie English, a former 42 Gang member and bodyguard to Sam Giancana, strolled out of the Amory Lounge and leaned up against the FBI observation car parked just across the street from the tavern. The agents reported, "English is bemoaning the fact that the federal government is closing in on the organization and nothing can be done about it. He made several bad remarks about the Kennedy administration and pointed out that the Attorney General raising money for the Cuba invaders makes Chicago's syndicate look like amateurs."

Business executives and CEOs across the country were whispering the same thing. Many of the executives were amazed to find themselves talking on the phone with the Attorney General of the United States and were even more amazed at what they heard. Kennedy operated shamelessly. He told businesses he wanted money for the Bay of Pigs program, and reminded them that they had either pending contracts before the government or criminal cases before the Justice Department. Before they could respond, Kennedy again mentioned the fund to free the Cubans, and hung up.

John Factor also knew about the fund to free the Cubans. In fact he threw $25,000 into the project and later explained to a curious press corp that James Roosevelt, the problem child of the clan, had approached him about the donation.[18]

---

18. James Roosevelt, then a member of Congress, strongly supported Factor's bid for a Presidential Pardon as well.

Factor had already given Kennedy $25,000 to help retire his campaign debt and his wife gave several thousand more. Despite the endless rumors to the contrary, Factor denied that he had given $1,000,000 to the Joseph P. Kennedy Foundation[19] as well.

Miraculously, on December 24, 1962, after Factor's contribution to the Bay of Pigs fund, President John F. Kennedy signed a presidential pardon for Factor for the mail fraud conviction. As a result the deportation proceeding against him was dismissed. For mob watchers and law enforcement employees, who had put so much faith in Robert Kennedy's war on crime, Jake the Barber's presidential pardon fell from the skies like a bolt of lightning.

It was never made clear if Kennedy's actions also killed the investigation of Factor's dealing in the Stardust but one way or the other, that investigation was closed.

Factor always denied that the mob used pressure with the White House to win him his pardon but in mid-1963, while Jake was trying to gain control of the National Life Insurance Company of America and was buying up the company's shares at $125 each, he sold 400 shares to Murray Humpreys at $20 each. Factor's loss was $105 per share. Humpreys then sold the shares back to Factor for $125 a share, making him $42,000 richer in one day.

As far as the Hump's unusual and creative stock

19. The Foundation refused this writer access to their records and refused to deny or confirm that Factor donated money to its treasury.

   The reader should note that the Foundation is a privately held trust; it does not have to account for its spending or explain salaries given to its executives, many of whom are, and have been members of the Kennedy family.

transaction with Jake[20] the Barber was concerned, the government decided that it was a taxable exchange "for services rendered" and sent capital gains tax bills to both of them.

A presidential pardon was good but just to be sure, on July 16, 1963, in Los Angeles, John Factor, the poor kid from the ghettos of Chicago, raised a slightly shaking hand and along with a dozen other more recent arrivals took the oath of citizenship of the United States of America. "I'm the luckiest man alive," he said and he was probably right.

• • •

John Factor died after a long illness at the age of ninety-one in 1984. More than 400 mourners, including California's Governor Pat Brown and Los Angeles Mayor Tom Bradley attended his wake.

During the last half of his long life Factor contributed millions to charitable causes and made serious efforts to change his life and his reputation, but nothing ever changed.

Once, after giving an enormous donation to a charity in the mid-sixties, the newspapers that covered the event wrote about Factor's shady past. The report brought on a rare display of public anger when Factor called the reporter on the story and demanded to know "What, my dear, must one do...how much does a man have to do...to bury his past?"

It was proof that despite his incredibly agile mind, John Factor either never really understood or refused to recognize the harm he had inflicted on others during his long life.

---

20. In 1960 an FBI informant, believed to be Jimmy "The Turk" recorded Humpreys and Joey Glimco discussing Roger Touhy's murder, a month after it happened. Humpreys said, "But this Factor, he's a dirty cocksucker...here's a guy I've always gone along with. We go ahead, and we do it, originally, and I wouldn't...so he says, ok...200,000." Its not clear from the transcripts if Humpreys was referring to a payment from Factor to him of $200,000 to murder Touhy. Humpreys added, "I had to give the cocksucker ten thousand dollars."

His stock swindle in England had fleeced thousands of people out of their life savings. His self-managed kidnapping had sent five innocent men to jail for a total of 125 years. The skim from the Stardust he helped to shelter produced an estimated $2,000,000 a year, net income, for each of the Chicago bosses who held points in the resort casino.

A better question would have been, "How much should a man pay before he is allowed to bury his past?"

• • •

In the end there were no winners, only losers. All that was left was the tragic tale of two men who willfully lived outside the law and then refused to accept the consequences of their actions. Up to their dying day, neither Roger Touhy nor John Factor would ever fully admit to wrongdoings in their lives or to the suffering they had created for others, including those who loved them.

Bibliography

Allen, Edward J. *Merchants of Menace—The Mafia*. Springfield, IL.: Charles C. Thomas, 1962.

Allsop, Kenneth. *The Bootleggers*. London: Hutchinson, 1961.

Anonymous. *Alcatraz*. San Francisco: E. Crowell Mensch, 1937.

Asbury, Herbert. *The Gangs of New York*. Garden City, N.J.: Garden City Publishing, 1928.

————*Gem of the Prairie: An Informal History of the Chicago Underworld*. New York: Alfred A. Knopf, 1940.

————*The Great Illusion: An Informal History of Prohibition*. New York: Doubleday & Co, 1950.

Bennett, James. "Chicago Gangland." *Chicago Tribune,* 1929.

Blakey, G. Robert and Richard N. Billings. *The Plot to Kill the President*. New York: Times Books, 1981.

Boettiger, John. *Jake Lingle*. New York: E.P. Dutton & Co., 1931.

Brill, Steven. *The Teamsters*. New York: Simon and Schuster, 1978.

Burns, Walter Noble. *The One Way Ride*. New York: Doubleday, 1931.

Busch, Francis X. *Enemies of the State*. New York: Bobbs-Merrill, 1954.

Churchill, Allen. *A Pictorial History of American Crime*. New York: Holt, Rinehart & Winston, 1964.

Cohen, Art. *The Joker is Wild: The Story of Joe E. Lewis*. New York: Random House, 1955.

Cooper, Courtney Ryley. *Ten Thousand Public Enemies*. New York: Blue Ribbon Books, 1935.

Cressey, Donald R. *Theft of a Nation*. New York: Harper & Row, 1969.

Dedmon, Emmet. *Fabulous Chicago*. New York: Random House, 1953.

Demaris, Ovid. *Captive City: Chicago in Chains*. New York: Lyle Stuart, 1969.

————*The Last Mafioso: The Treacherous World of Jimmy Fratianno*. New York: Times Books, 1981.

Dobyns, Fletcher. *The Underworld of American Politics*. Self published, 1932.

Dorman, Michael. *Payoff: The Role of Organized Crime in American Politics*. New York: David McKay & Co., 1972.

Ellis, Steve. *Alcatraz Number 1172*. Los Angeles: Holloway House Publishing, 1969.

Feder, Sid. *The Luciano Story*. New York: David McKay & Co., 1954.

Fried, Albert. *The Rise and Fall of the Jewish Gangster in America*. New York: Holt, Rinehart and Winston, 1980.

Gosch, Martin A. *The Last Testament of Lucky Luciano*. Boston: Little Brown and Company, 1975.

Hearings before the Permanent Subcommittee on Investigation. Organized Crime and Illicit Traffic in Narcotics. U.S. Senate, 1963.

Hearings before the Special Committee to Investigate Organized Crime in Interstate Commerce. U.S. Senate, 1950.

Helmer, William J. *The Gun That Made the Twenties Roar*. New York: Macmillan Co., 1969.

Hutchinson, John. *The Imperfect Union: A History of Corruption in American Trade Unions*. New York: E.P. Dutton & Co., 1972.

Irey, Elmer J. *The Tax Dodgers*. Garden City, N.J.: Garden City Publishing Co., 1948.

Johnston, James A. *Alcatraz Island Prison*. New York: Charles Scribner & Sons, 1949.

Katcher, Leo. *The Big Bankroll: The Life and Times of Arnold Rothstein*. New York: Harper & Brothers, 1959.

Katz, Leonard. *Uncle Frank: The Biography of Frank Costello*. New York: Drake, 1973.

Kavanagh, Marcus. *The Criminal and His Allies*. Indianapolis, Ind.: Bobbs-Merrill, 1928.

——*You Be the Judge*. Chicago: Reilly & Lee, 1929.

Keating, W.J., and Carter, R. *The Man Who Rocked the Boat*. New York: Harper, 1956.

Kefauver, Estes. *Crime in America*. New York: Doubleday, 1951.

——*In a Few Hands*. New York: Pantheon, 1965.

——*Second Interim Report*. Washington, D.C.: U.S. Government Printing Office, 1951.

——*Third Interim Report*. Washington D.C.: U.S. Government Printing Office, 1951.

——and Levin, Jack. *A 20th Century Congress*. New York: Duell Sloan, 1947.

Kefauver Committee Report on Organized Crime. New York: Didier, 1951.

Kelley, Clarence M. *Crime in the United States, 1976*. Washington, D.C.: U.S. Government Printing Office, 1977.

Kelly, Jack. *On the Street*. Chicago: Henry Regnery, 1974.

Kelly, Robert J., ed. *Organized Crime: An International Perspective*. Totowa, N.J.: Rowman & Littlefield, 1986.

Kennedy, Robert F. *The Enemy Within*. New York: Popular Library, 1960.

Keylin, Arleen, and DeMirjian, Arto, Jr. *Crime: As Reported by the New York Times*. New York: Arno Press, 1976.

——*The Fabulous Fifties*. New York: Arno Press, 1978.

Kilian, Michael, Connie Fletcher, and Ciccone Richard F. *Who Runs Chicago?* New York: St. Martin's Press, 1979.

Kilroe, Edwin P. *Saint Tammany and the Origin of the Society of Tammany or Columbian Order in the City of New York*. New York: M.B. Brown, 1913.

King, Rufus. *The Drug Hang-Up: America's Fifty Year Folly*. New York: W.W. Norton, 1972.

——*Gambling and Organized Crime*. Washington, D.C.: Public Affairs Press, 1969.

King, Veronica and Paul King. *Problems of Modern American Crime*. London: Heath Cranton, 1924.

Kinney, Jay, and Paul Mavrides. *Cover-Up Lowdown*. San Francisco: Rip Off Press, 1977.

Kinsley, Philip. *The Chicago Tribune: Its First Hundred Years*. Chicago: Chicago Tribune, 1943.

Kirby, Cecil, and Thomas C. Renner. *Mafia Enforcer*. New York: Villard Books, 1987.

Kirkland, Joseph. *The Story of Chicago*. Chicago: Dibble, 1892.

Kirkpatrick, Ernest E. *Crime's Paradise*. San Antonio, TX.: Naylor, 1934.

———*Voices From Alcatraz*. San Antonio, TX.: Naylor, 1947.

Kitson, Frank. *Bunch of Five*. London: Faber & Faber, 1977.

———*Gangs and Counter-Gangs*. London: Barrie & Rockliffe, 1960.

Klein, Alexander, ed. *Double Dealers*. Philadelphia and New York: J.B. Lippincott, 1958.

Klein, Felix. In the Land of the Strenuous Life. Chicago: A.C. McClurg, 1905.

Klein, Herbert T. *The Police*. New York: Crown, 1968.

Klein, Malcolm W. *Juvenile Gangs in Context*. Englewood Cliffs, N.J.: Prentice-Hall, 1967.

———*Street Gangs and Street Workers*. Englewood Cliffs, N.J.: Prentice -Hall, 1971.

Klockars, Carl B. *The Professional Fence*. New York: Free Press, 1974.

Klurfeld, Herman. *Winchell: His Life and Times*. New York: Frederick A. Praeger, 1976.

Knapp, Whitman. *Knapp Commission Report on Police Corruption*. New York: George Brazilier, 1972.

Knox, Thomas W. *Underground, or Life Below the Surface*. Hartford, C.: J.B. Burr & Hyde, 1873.

Knudten, Richard D. *Crime in a Complex Society: An Introduction to Criminology*. New York: Dorsey Press, 1970.

———, ed. *Criminal Controversies*. New York: Appleton-Century-Crofts, 1968.

Kobler, John. *Ardent Spirits: The Rise and Fall of Prohibition*. New York: G.P. Putnam's Sons, 1973.

——— *Capone: The Life and World of Al Capone*. New York: G.P. Putnam's Sons, 1971.

Kogan, Herman and Lloyd Wendt. *Chicago: A Pictorial History*. New York: E.P. Dutton, 1958.

Kogan, Herman and and Rick Kogan. *Yesterday's Chicago*. Miami, FL.: E.A. Seemann, 1976.

Krout, John Allen. *The Origins of Prohibition*. New York: Alfred A. Knopf, 1925.

Kwitney, Jonathan. *Vicious Circles: The Mafia in the Marketplace*. New York: W.W. Norton, 1979.

Lait, Jack and Lee Mortimer. *Chicago Confidential*. New York: Crown, 1950.

——— *New York Confidential*. Chicago: Ziff-Davis, 1948.

——— *U.S.A. Confidential*. Crown, 1952.

——— *Washington Confidential*. New York: Crown, 1951.

Lamb, Martha and Burton Harrison. *History of the City of New York.* New York: A.S. Barnes, 1877.

Lamour, Catherine and Michael R. Lamberti, *The International Connection: Opium From Growers to Pushers.* New York: Pantheon, 1974.

Landesco, John. *Organized Crime in Chicago.* Chicago: University of Chicago Press, 1968.

Lane, Roger. *Policing the City: Boston, 1822-1885.* Cambridge, MA: Harvard University Press, 1967.

Lee, Henry. *How Dry We Were: Prohibition Revisited.* Englewood Cliffs, N.J.: Prentice-Hall, 1963.

Lee, Raymond and B.C. Van Hecke. *Gangsters and Hoodlums: The Underworld and the Cinema.* New York: Barnes & Noble, 1971.

Leiter, Robert D. *The Teamsters Union.* New York: Bookman Associates, 1957.

Lening, Gustav. *The Dark Side of New York Life.* New York: F. Gerhard, 1873.

Lens, Sydney. *The Labor Wars.* Garden City, N.Y.: Doubleday, 1974.

Le Shan, Edna. *The Roots of Crime.* New York: Four Winds Press, 1981.

Lever, Harry and Joseph Young. *Wartime Racketeers.* New York: G.P. Putnam's Sons, 1945.

Levine, Gary. *Anatomy of a Gangster.* New York: Barnes, 1979.

Lewis, Alfred Henry. *The Apaches of New York.* New York: G.W. Dillingham, 1912.

——— *The Boss: And How He Came to Rule New York.* New York: A.S. Barnes, 1903.

——— *Richard Croker.* New York: Life, 1901.

Lewis, Dioclesian. *Prohibition, a Failure.* Boston: James R. Osgood, 1875.

Lewis, Jerry D. *Crusade Against Crime.* New York: Bernard Geis Associates, 1962.

Lewis, Lloyd and Henry Justin Smith. *Chicago: The History of Its Reputation.* New York: Harcourt, Brace, 1929.

Lewis, Norman. *The Honored Society.* New York: G.P. Putnam's Sons, 1964.

Lewis, Sasha G. *American Exploitation of Illegal Aliens.* Boston: Beacon Press, 1979.

Lindberg, Richard C. *Chicago Ragtime: Another Look at Chicago, 1880-1920.* South Bend, IN: Icarus Press, 1985.

——— *To Serve and Collect: Chicago Politics and Police Corruption from the Lager Beer Riot to the Summerdale Scandal: 1855-1960.* New York: Praeger Press, 1991.

——— *Who's On Third?: The Chicago White Sox Story.* South Bend, IN: Icarus Press, 1983.

Lindsey, Benjamin B. and Harvey J. O'Higgins. *The Beast.* New York: Doubleday, Page, 1911.

Linn, James Weber. *James Keeley, Newspaperman.* Indianapolis: Bobbs-Merrill, 1937.

Linton, Calvin D. ed. *American Headlines Year by Year*. New York: Thomas Nelson, 1985.

Lloyd, Benjamin Estelle. *Lights and Shadows in San Francisco*. San Francisco: Self published, 1876.

———— *Lights and Shadows of Chinatown*. San Francisco: Self published, 1896.

Longstreet, Stephen. *All Star Cast, an Anecdotal History of Los Angeles*. New York: Thomas Y. Crowell, 1977.

———— *Chicago, 1860-1919*. New York: McKay, 1973.

———— *Sportin' House*. Los Angeles: Sherbourne Press, 1965.

———— *The Wilder Shore*. New York: Doubleday, 1968.

———— *Win or Lose*. Indianapolis: Bobbs-Merrill, 1977.

Lowe, David. *Lost Chicago*. Boston: Houghton Mifflin, 1975.

Lowenthal, Max. *The Federal Bureau of Investigation*. New York: William Sloane Associates, 1950.

Lyle, John H. *The Dry and Lawless Years*. Englewood Cliffs, N.J.: Prentice-Hall, 1960.

Maas, Peter. *Serpico*. New York: Viking Press, 1973.

———— *The Valachi Papers*. New York: G.P. Putnam's Sons, 1968.

McBain, Howard Lee. *Prohibition: Legal and Illegal*. New York: Macmillan, 1928.

McCabe, James D. *Lights and Shadow of New York Life*. Philadephia: National, 1872.

McCaghy, C.H. *Crime in American Society*. New York: Macmillan, 1980.

McClellan, John L. *Crime without Punishment*. New York: Duell, Sloan & Pearce, 1962.

McConaughy, John. *From Cain to Capone: Racketeering Down the Ages*. New York: Brentano's, 1931.

McCord, W. and J. McCord. *Origins of Crime*. New York: Columbia University Press, 1959.

MacDougall, Ernest D. ed. *Crime for Profit: A Symposium on Mercenary Crime*. Boston: Statford, 1933.

McIlvaine, Mabel, ed. *Reminiscences of Chicago during the Civil War*. Chicago: R.R. Donnelley, 1914.

———— ed. *Reminiscences of Chicago during the Forties and Fifties*. Chicago: R.R. Donnelley, 1913.

———— *Reminiscences of Early Chicago*. Chicago: Lakeside Press, 1912.

McIntosh, Arthur T. *Chicago*. Chicago: Press of G.G. Renneker, 1921.

McIntosh, Mary. *The Organization of Crime*. London: Macmillan, 1975.

Mack, John A. *The Crime Industry*. Westmead, England: Saxon House, 1974.

Mackay, Margaret. *Los Angeles Proper and Improper*. New York: Goodwin, 1938.

McKean, Dayton. *The Boss*. Boston: Houghton Mifflin, 1940.

McPhaul, John J. *Johnny Torrio*. New Rochelle, N.Y.: Arlington House, 1970.

Mandelbaum, Seymour J. *Boss Tweed's New York*. New York: John Wiley & Sons, 1965.

Mann, Arthur. *La Guardia Comes to Power: 1933*. Philadelphia: J.B. Lippincott, 1965.

Marsh, Thomas O. *Roots of Crime*. Newton, N.J.: Nellen, 1981.

Martienssen, Anthony. *Crime and the Police*. London: Martin Secker & Warbury, 1951.

Martin, John Bartlow. *Break Down the Walls*. New York: Ballantine, 1954

——— *My Life in Crime*. New York: Harper & Brothers, 1952.

Martin, Ralph G. *Ballots and Bandwagons*. Chicago: Rand McNally, 1964.

Martin, Raymond V. *Revolt in the Mafia*. New York: Duell, 1963.

Marye, George Thomas. *Secrets of the Great City; the Virtues and the Vices, the Mysteries, Miseries and Crimes at New York City*. New York: Self published, 1968.

Mason, Edward Gay, ed. *Early Chicago and Illinois*. Chicago: Fergus Printing, 1890.

Mayhew, Henry. *London's Underworld*. London: William Kimber, 1950.

Meeker, Arthur. *Chicago With Love*. New York: Alfred A. Knopf, 1955.

Mensch, Earnest Cromwell. *Alcatraz*. San Francisco: San Francisco, 1937.

Merriam, Charles Edward. *Chicago: A More Intimate View of Urban Politics*. Chicago: University of Chicago Press, 1929.

Merz, Charles. *The Dry Decade*. New York: Doubleday, Doran, 1931.

——— *The Great American Bandwagon*. New York: John Day, 1928.

Meskil, Paul S., with Callahan. *Gerard M. Cheesebox*. Englewood Cliffs, N.J.: Prentice-Hall, 1974.

——— *Don Carlo: Boss of Bosses*. New York: Popular Library, 1973.

——— *John Edgar Hoover*. New York: David McKay, 1972.

——— *Lansky*. New York: G.P. Putnam's Sons, 1971.

——— *The Mobs and the Mafia*. New York: Ballantine Books.

——— *Of Grass and Snow: The Secret Criminal Elite*. Englewood Cliffs, N.J.: Prentice-Hall, 1979.

——— *The Only Game in Town*. New York: T.Y. Crowell, 1976.

——— *The Politics of Prosecution*. Ottawa, IL: Caroline House Books, 1978.

——— *The Private Lives of Public Enemies*. New York: P.H. Wyden, 1973.

——— *Secret File*. New York: G.P. Putnam's Sons, 1969.

——— *The Silent Syndicate*. New York: Macmillan, 1967.

——— *Syndicate in the Sun*. New York: Macmillan, 1968.

Milligan, Maurice M. T*he Inside Story of the Pendergast Machine by the Man Who Smashed It*. New York: Charles Scribner's Sons, 1948.

——— *Missouri Waltz*. New York: Charles Scribner's Sons, 1948.

Mills, James. *The Prosecutor*. New York: Pocket Books, 1970.

——— *The Underground Empire: Where Crime and Governments Meet*. New York: Dell, 1986.

Millspaugh, Arthur. *Crime Control by the National Government.* Washington, D.C.: Brookings, 1937.

Minnigerode, Meade. *The Fabulous Forties 1840-1850.* Garden City, N.Y.: Garden City, 1924.

Mitchell, John. *Organized Labor.* Philadelphia: American Book and Bible House, 1903.

Moldea, Dan E. *The Hoffa Wars.* New York: Charter Books, 1978.

Monaghan, Frank and Marvin Lowenthal. *This was New York.* New York: Doubleday, Doran, 1943.

Mooney, M. *Crime Incorporated.* New York: McGraw-Hill, 1935.

—— *Crime, Unincorporated.* New York: Whittlesey House, 1935.

Mooney-Billings Report Suppressed by the Wickersham Commission. New York: Gotham House, 1932.

Moore, Robin with Barbara Fuca. *Mafia Wife.* New York: Macmillan, 1977.

Moore, William H. *The Kefauver Committee and the Politics of Crime.* Columbia: University of Missouri Press, 1974.

Moore, William T. *Dateline Chicago.* New York: Taplinger, 1973.

Moquin, Wayne. *The American Way of Crime.* New York: Frederick A. Praeger, 1976.

Morain, Alfred. *The Underground of Paris.* New York: Blue Ribbon Books, 1931.

Moray, Alastair. *The Diary of a Rum Runner.* London: Philip, Alan, 1929.

Morgan, John. *Prince of Crime.* New York: Stein and Day, 1985.

Mori, Cesare. *The Last Struggle of the Mafia.* Translated by Orlo Williams. New York: G.P. Putnam's Sons, 1933.

Morris, Lloyd R. *Incredible New York.* New York: Random House, 1951.

—— *Not So Long Ago.* New York: Random House, 1949.

—— *Postscript to Yesterday.* New York: Random House, 1947.

Morris, Norval. *The Habitual Criminal.* Cambridge, MA: Harvard University Press, 1951.

Moses, John and Joseph Kirkland. *History of Chicago.* 2 vols. Chicago: Munsell, 1895.

Moss, Frank. *The American Metropolis, From Knickerbocker Days to the Present Time, New York City Life in All Its Various Phases.* 3 vols. New York: Peter Fenelon Collier, 1897.

Muir, Helen. *Miami, U.S.A.* New York: Holt, 1953.

Murray, George. *The Legacy of Al Capone.* New York: Putnam, 1975.

Mushkat, Jerome. *Tammany: The Evolution of a Political Machine, 1789-1865.* Syracuse, N.Y.: Syracuse University Press, 1971.

Myers, Gustavus. *History of Tammany Hall.* New York: Boni & Liveright, 1901.

National Commission on Law Observance and Enforcement. Report on the Enforcement of the Prohibition Laws of the Laws of the U.S., 193. New York: Drake Publishers, 1973.

Needham, Ted and Howard Needham. *Alcatraz.* Millbrae, CA: Celestial Arts, 1976.

Nelli, Humbert S. *The Business of Crime: Italians and Syndicate*

Crime in the United States. New York: Oxford University Press, 1976.

Ness, Eliot with Oscar Fraley. *The Untouchables.* New York: Julian Messner, 1957.

Newell, Barbara W. *Chicago and the Labor Movement: Metropolitan Unionism in the 1930s.* Urbana: University of Illinois Press, 1961.

Northrup, William B. and John B. Northrup. *The Insolence of Office: The Story of the Seabury Investigation.* New York: G.P. Putnam's Sons, 1932.

O'Connor, John J. *Broadway Racketeers.* New York: Liveright, 1928.

O'Connor, Len. *Clout: Mayor Daley and His City.* Chicago: Henry Regnery, 1974.

O'Connor, Richard. *Hell's Kitchen.* Philadelphia: J.B. Lippincott, 1958.

Ollestad, Norman. *Inside the FBI.* New York: Lancer, 1968.

Ostermann, Robert. *Crime in America.* New York: Dow Jones, 1966.

Ostrander, Gilman M. *The Prohibition Movement in California, 1848-1933.* Los Angeles: University of California Press, 1957.

Ottenberg, Miriam. *The Federal Investigators.* Englewood Cliffs, N.J.: Prentice-Hall, 1962.

Overstreet, Harry A. and Bonaro Overstreet. *The FBI in an Open Society.* New York: W.W. Norton, 1969.

Palmer, Vivien M. *Social Backgrounds of Chicago's Local Communities.* Chicago: University of Chicago Press, 1930.

Pantaleone, Michele. *The Mafia and Politics.* New York: Coward-McCann, 1966.

Park, Robert E., Ernest W. Burgess, and Roderick D. MacKensie. *The City.* Chicago: University of Chicago Press, 1925.

Perlman, Selig and Philip Taft. *History of Labor in the United States 1896-1932.* New York: Macmillan, 1935.

Perrett, Geoffrey. *America in the Twenties.* New York: Simon & Schuster, 1982.

Petacco, Arrigo. *Joe Petrosino.* New York: Macmillan, 1974.

Peters, Charles and Taylor Branch. *Blowing the Whistle.* New York: Frederick A. Praeger, 1972.

Petersen, David M. and Marcello Truzzi eds. *Criminal Life: Views from the Inside.* Englewood Cliffs, N.J.: Prentice-Hall, 1972.

Peterson, Virgil W. *Barbarians in Our Midst: A History of Chicago Crime and Politics.* Boston: Little, Brown, 1952.

——— *Crime Commissions in the United States.* Chicago: Chicago Crime Commission, 1945.

——— *The Mob: 200 Years of Organized Crime in New York.* Ottawa, IL: Green Hill, 1983.

——— *A Report on Chicago Crime for 1956.* Chicago: Chicago Crime Commission, 1957.

——— *A Report on Chicago Crime for 1958.* Chicago: Chicago Crime Commission, 1959.

——— *A Report on Chicago Crime for 1961.* Chicago: Chicago Crime Commission, 1962.

—— *A Report on Chicago Crime for 1963.* Chicago: Chicago Crime Commission, 1964.

—— *A Report on Chicago Crime for 1965.* Chicago: Chicago Crime Commission, 1966.

—— *A Report on Chicago Crime for 1967.* Chicago: Chicago Crime Commission, 1968.

Pickering, Clarence R. *The Early Days of Prohibition.* New York: Vantage Press, 1964.

Pierce, Bessie Louise. *As Others See Chicago: Impressions of Visitors, 1673-1933.* Chicago: University of Chicago Press, 1932.

—— *A History of Chicago.* 3 vols. New York: Alfred A. Knopf, 1937.

Plate, Thomas. *Crime Pays!* New York: Simon and Schuster, 1975.

—— *The Mafia at War.* New York: Magazine Press, 1972.

Ploscowe, Morris. *Organized Crime and Law Enforcement.* New York: Grosby Press, 1952-53.

Plumbe, George E. *Chicago.* Chicago: Chicago Association of Commerce, 1912.

Plunkitt, George W. *Plunkitt of Tammany Hall.* New York: Alfred A. Knopf, 1948.

Prall, Robert H., and Norton Mockridge. *This is Costello.* New York: Gold Medal Books, 1951.

Putterman, Jaydie, and Rosalyn Lesur. *Police.* New York: Holt, Rinehart & Winston, 1983.

Quinby, G.W. *The Gallows, the Prison and the Poor House.* Cincinnati, OH: Quinby, 1856.

Rakov, Milton L. *Don't Make No Waves, Don't Back No Losers.* Bloomington: Indiana University Press, 1975.

Reckless, Walter. *American Criminology: New Directions.* New York: Appleton-Century-Crofts, 1973.

—— *The Crime Problem.* New York: D. Appleton, 1950.

—— *Vice in Chicago.* Chicago: University of Chicago Press, 1933.

Reed, Lear B. *Human Wolves: Seventeen Years of War on Crime.* Kansas City, MO: Brown-White, Lowell Press, 1941.

Reid, Ed and Ovid DeMaris. *The Green Felt Jungle.* New York: Trident Press, 1964.

—— *The Grim Reapers, The Anatomy of Organized Crime in America.* Chicago: Henry Regnery, 1969.

—— *Mafia.* New York: Random House, 1952.

—— *The Mistress and the Mafia.* New York: Bantam, 1972.

—— *The Shame of New York.* New York: Random House, 1953.

Reisman, W. Michael. *Folded Lies: Bribery, Crusades, and Reforms.* New York: Free Press, 1979.

Reuter, Peter. *Disorganized Crime.* Cambridge, MA: Massachusetts Institute of Technology, 1983.

Rice, Robert. *The Business of Crime.* New York: Farrar, Straus & Cudahy, 1956.

Robinson, W.W. *Bombs and Bribery.* Los Angeles: 1969.

—— *Lawyers of Los Angeles.* Los Angeles: Los Angeles Bar Association, 1959.

Roeburt, John. *Al Capone.* New York: Pyramid, 1959.

Rosow, Eugene. *Born to Lose, the Gangster Film in America.* New York: Oxford University Press, 1978.

Ross, Robert. *The Trial of Al Capone.* Chicago: Robert Ross, 1933.

Rovere, Richard H. *Howe and Hummell: Their True and Scandalous History.* New York: Farrar, Straus, 1947.

Royko, Mike. *Boss: Richard J. Daley of Chicago.* New York: E.P. Dutton, 1971.

Rudensky, Morris ("Red") and Don Riley. *The Gonif.* Blue Earth, MN: Piper, 1970.

Acknowledgements

To Alan Wilson, my guide and editor at Barricade Books, who worked diligently to make a good book better. And to Barricade's President, Lyle Stuart, who continues to encourage new writers and take chances on books that need to written.

***

Bill "Eagle Eye" Cricthley, my editor at The Magazine Network who works patiently decodes my spelling mistakes and making my work readable.

***

Lieutenant Douglas "Happy" Moran, of Waterbury, Connecticut for encouragement in the early stages of my research to continued writing.

***

Wayne Johnson, chief investigator of the Chicago Crime Commission for accurate insights and more than a few laughs.

***

Rick Porrello, author, crime historian and founder of American Mafia.Com, and that site's editor, Thomas Michael Basie, for their help in promoting my writing.

***

Josh Erikson at Mob Central.Com.

***

Dennis Menos whose insights and experience in the book's preperation were priceless

***

And, of course, to my sisters Florence, Christine and Kathleen and my brothers Paul and Danny. To the memory of my brother, James, and all of my nieces and nephews. There are few people I respect more, or whose respect I would rather have.